Dear Reader,

You and I have been living through challenging times. I went from being busy to having too much time on my hands. I used the extra time during the height of the COVID-19 pandemic to focus on the things that I love to do, like cooking for myself once again.

From a prolonged lockdown was born *The Everything® Green Mediterranean Cookbook*, following the dietary and lifestyle philosophy of the diet but concentrating on its essence: consuming a **plant-based diet** with legumes, good fats, whole grains, nuts, and only a sparse amount of meat.

You will not find any dishes with red meat in this cookbook, but there are plenty of nutritious (and delicious) dishes with poultry, seafood, and, of course, plant-based main courses.

The goal of this book is to provide those looking to lose weight and **improve their overall physical well-being** with two hundred recipes suited to these purposes.

My long-term goal has been to reduce my consumption of meat, and the green Mediterranean diet helps with that goal—along with the shedding of a few pounds.

This past year has been full of challenges, but I am happy to rise to the occasion and present a subject which I love (food), and offer delicious, **easy-to-cook dishes** that will help you on your journey to better physical wellness.

Peter Minaki

Welcome to the Everything® Series!

These handy, accessible books give you all you need to tackle a difficult project, gain a new hobby, comprehend a fascinating topic, prepare for an exam, or even brush up on something you learned back in school but have since forgotten.

You can choose to read an Everything® book from cover to cover or just pick out the information you want from our four useful boxes: Questions, Facts, Alerts, and Essentials. We give you everything you need to know on the subject, but throw in a lot of fun stuff along the way too.

question
Answers to common questions.

fact
Important snippets of information.

alert
Urgent warnings.

essential
Quick handy tips.

We now have more than 600 Everything® books in print, spanning such wide-ranging categories as cooking, health, parenting, personal finance, wedding planning, word puzzles, and so much more. When you're done reading them all, you can finally say you know Everything®!

PUBLISHER Karen Cooper

MANAGING EDITOR Lisa Laing

COPY CHIEF Casey Ebert

PRODUCTION EDITOR Jo-Anne Duhamel

ACQUISITIONS EDITOR Lisa Laing

SENIOR DEVELOPMENT EDITOR Lisa Laing

EVERYTHING® SERIES COVER DESIGNER Erin Alexander

THE EVERYTHING®

GREEN

MEDITERRANEAN

COOKBOOK

PETER MINAKI

200 PLANT-BASED RECIPES FOR HEALTHY—AND SATISFYING—WEIGHT LOSS

ADAMS MEDIA

NEW YORK   LONDON   TORONTO   SYDNEY   NEW DELHI

Aadams media

Adams Media
An Imprint of Simon & Schuster, Inc.
100 Technology Center Drive
Stoughton, Massachusetts 02072

An Everything® Series Book.

First Adams Media trade paperback edition November 2021

ADAMS MEDIA and colophon are trademarks of Simon & Schuster.

For information about special discounts for bulk purchases, please contact Simon & Schuster Special Sales at 1-866-506-1949 or business@simonandschuster.com.

The Simon & Schuster Speakers Bureau can bring authors to your live event. For more information or to book an event contact the Simon & Schuster Speakers Bureau at 1-866-248-3049 or visit our website at www.simonspeakers.com.

Interior design by Colleen Cunningham
Photographs by James Stefiuk

Manufactured in the United States of America

1 2021

Library of Congress Cataloging-in-Publication Data
Names: Minaki, Peter, author.
Title: The everything® green Mediterranean cookbook / Peter Minaki.
Description: Stoughton, MA: Adams Media, 2021. | Series: Everything® | Includes index.
Identifiers: LCCN 2021032918 | ISBN 9781507216620 (pb) | ISBN 9781507216637 (ebook)
Subjects: LCSH: Cooking, Mediterranean. | Vegetarian cooking. | LCGFT: Cookbooks.
Classification: LCC TX725.M35 M548 2021 | DDC 641.59/1822--dc23
LC record available at https://lccn.loc.gov/2021032918

ISBN 978-1-5072-1662-0
ISBN 978-1-5072-1663-7 (ebook)

Contains material adapted from the following title published by Adams Media, an Imprint of Simon & Schuster, Inc.: *The Everything® Healthy Mediterranean Cookbook* by Peter Minaki, copyright © 2019, ISBN 978-1-5072-1150-2.

Contents

Introduction

The Mediterranean region is known for its beauty, diversity, variety of seafoods, and the diet that takes its name from the region that encompasses the countries surrounding the Mediterranean Sea. Despite the wide range of countries that comprise the Mediterranean region, the Mediterranean diet is most commonly associated with Spain, southern France, Italy, Greece, and the Middle East. There are regional differences in what constitutes the Mediterranean diet, but all share an essential common trait: a focus on whole grains, fruits, vegetables, and fish.

Although the Mediterranean diet has been enjoyed for centuries, within the last sixty years it has been the subject of much interest by dietitians, medical professionals, and consumers. People in the southern Mediterranean countries tend to have less heart disease compared to those in Western Europe and North America, even though they consume more fat than many dietary guidelines recommend and drink a relatively large amount of wine. These two factors seem to contradict the precepts of healthful eating, but for people in the Mediterranean this diet is a part of life. Another factor that characterizes this diet is the use of oils, nuts, and seeds. The use of certain oils—monounsaturated "healthful fats"—in place of animal fats provides a variety of phytonutrients, which help in the prevention of disease.

Recently, scientists have begun to study ways to make the Mediterranean diet, already one of the best diets on the planet, an even more effective plan for weight loss and improved health. A 2020 medical study found that participants who ate a Mediterranean diet lost more weight than others who followed a traditionally "healthy" diet. And those who followed a Green Mediterranean diet lost the most weight of all. This Green Mediterranean diet adds a few tweaks to the traditional

Mediterranean eating plan. Participants cut out meat and most meat products and added three things to their daily diet: a high-protein green smoothie, 3 to 4 cups of green tea, and a handful of walnuts.

Whether you're following the Green Mediterranean or the traditional Mediterranean diet, in this cookbook you'll find hundreds of recipes to inspire you. Start the day with a hearty Mediterranean Omelet (Chapter 2) and a cup of green tea. For lunch, choose from colorful salads like Romaine Salad with Fennel, Orange, and Olives (Chapter 5), a Hummus Power Bowl (Chapter 4), or a simple Chickpea Soup (Chapter 7). You'll also find lots of ideas for expanding your weeknight dinner repertoire, from Penne all'Arrabbiata (Chapter 9) to Imam Bayildi (Turkish Stuffed Eggplant) (Chapter 6). And of course, there are many options for green smoothies packed with plant-based protein.

No matter which recipe you choose, take a cue from the people of the Mediterranean region—take a break and savor your meal and the company of others. Taking time to smell, taste, and savor the flavors of a meal improves the feelings of satisfaction and enjoyment. As you embark on this journey into healthier eating, think about the excitement new foods can provide and shift your food choices to a more plant-based diet that emphasizes vegetables, dried beans and peas, fruits, whole grains, nuts, and seeds. Healthy eating has never been more delicious!

CHAPTER 1
A Plant-Based Plan for Healthy Weight Loss

While there may be as many Mediterranean diets as there are countries in the Mediterranean, all of the diets from the region have one thing in common: They build meals around plant foods and most often enjoy them in their whole form. Vegetables, fruits, legumes, whole grains, and healthy fats take center stage, while animal products serve as supporting players. Tweak that diet—remove red meat, limit other animal proteins, and add some high-quality plant proteins—and you have the Green Mediterranean diet, which has been found to be more effective in improving health and weight loss.

The Healthiest Diet on the Planet

Studies show that in comparison to consumers of the traditional Western diet, the people of the Mediterranean live longer, weigh less, and suffer from fewer medical complaints, such as cardiovascular disease. Researchers looked at their lifestyles and found that the key to their abundant good health was their diet, their activity level, and the amount of time they spent with friends and family. They don't count calories, they don't deprive themselves, and they don't believe in bland meals.

What does all this mean? The Mediterranean diet is a heart-healthy eating plan that focuses on fresh, plant-based meals, healthy fats, and whole grains. Meals are made up of vegetables, whole grains, legumes, pulses (beans, lentils, and peas), pasta, fresh fruit, nuts, and rice. Healthy fats (such as olive oil) replace other fats (such as butter), dairy products are eaten in moderation, and fresh herbs and spices are used more than salt. Seafood is enjoyed occasionally—roughly two or three servings of fish or other seafood a week—while poultry is eaten about once a week, and red meat limited to one to two servings a month.

Even without restricting the amount of food you eat, consuming the foods of the Mediterranean can help you to lose weight. Combining the diet with a reduction in your daily calorie intake makes weight loss even more likely.

The Mediterranean diet encourages lifestyle changes in addition to dietary changes. The first is to add physical activity into your day. Take a long walk before or after dinner, participate in sports, or even just take the stairs at work instead of the elevator. Adding more movement into your daily routine will improve your health and your mood.

> **fact**
>
> A Nurses' Health Study (*Annals of Internal Medicine*, 2013) followed more than 10,000 women and found that those who followed a Mediterranean eating plan were 46 percent more likely to reach age 70 without chronic diseases like type 2 diabetes, kidney disease, lung disease, Parkinson's disease, and cancer, and without major declines in cognitive and physical function. The women who aged healthfully consumed more plant-based foods, whole grains, and fish; fewer processed and red meats; and a moderate amount of alcohol.

Another mood enhancer is to slow down and enjoy your meals with friends and family. Spend time talking, pausing while you eat to enjoy the company of those around you. Finally, drink more water. The Mediterranean diet encourages staying hydrated with water or unsweetened drinks like coffee or tea. Sugary drinks, like juice or sodas, should be avoided. These changes may seem small, but they can have a big impact on your health over time.

The Green Mediterranean Diet

The results of a November 2020 study on the effectiveness of the Mediterranean diet was published in the health journal *Heart*. Researchers compared three groups of individuals who were all defined as sedentary and moderately obese (with a BMI of about 31). All of the participants were provided with guidance to increase their daily activity. One group was instructed to eat a healthy diet in addition to the exercise. A second group was advised to follow the traditional Mediterranean diet with daily calorie limits of 1,200–1,400 for women and 1,500–1,800 for men. The third group was given guidelines to follow a Green Mediterranean diet with the same calorie restrictions.

---

question

What is mankai?

Duckweed, a tiny flowering plant, is a nutritional powerhouse. The cultivated version of duckweed is called Mankai, and you can buy it in frozen 100-gram cubes. Three cubes can be dropped into a smoothie to boost its nutritional profile to impressive levels. A complete protein with all nine essential amino acids, Mankai has no cholesterol or added sugar and is very low in sodium. One serving provides 45 calories, 1 gram of total fat, 5 grams of carbohydrates, 4 grams of fiber, and 5 grams of protein. It's an excellent source of folate, zinc, iron, and vitamins A and K.

Both versions of the Mediterranean diet followed in the study eliminated red meat and processed meats and added a daily snack of a handful of walnuts; the Green Mediterranean diet added 3–4 cups of green tea per day and a plant-based smoothie containing frozen cubes of Mankai duckweed, an aquatic plant rich in protein, iron, and other nutrients.

After six months, those on either Mediterranean diet lost more weight than those in the "healthy diet" group, who lost an average of 3.3 pounds. The Mediterranean dieters lost 11.5 pounds, and the Green Mediterranean dieters lost 13.7 pounds. The Green Mediterranean group also reduced their levels of "bad" cholesterol by nearly 4 percent, and they recorded reductions in blood pressure, insulin resistance, and inflammation. All of these factors are known to decrease the risk of heart disease.

The Green Mediterranean Diet is relatively easy to follow. The daily green smoothie and walnuts make satisfying snacks, and the list of foods you should eat is varied and vibrant:

- Green tea
- Water
- Mankai cubes or a plant-based protein powder
- Nonstarchy vegetables, such as broccoli, green beans, cauliflower, and onions
- Leafy greens
- Tomatoes
- Fruit

- Eggs
- Cottage cheese
- Yogurt
- Almonds
- Walnuts
- Olive oil
- Tahini
- Herbs and spices
- Fish and poultry (in limited amounts)

And the list of foods to avoid is short:

- Red meat
- Processed meat
- Highly processed foods (snack foods like chips, crackers, and cereals)
- Desserts
- Soda and other sweetened beverages

The best way to approach any diet is to focus on what you should be eating rather than what you shouldn't. The staples of the Mediterranean diet are fresh, satisfying, and, most of all, delicious. Take the time to add the healthiest foods to your daily diet to replace processed and packaged foods. Here are some things to try as you make the transition to a better, healthier lifestyle:

- Increase your intake of legumes and beans. Canned products make this easier.
- Eat vegetables and fruits at every meal. At least half your plate should be produce.
- Add 1 ounce of walnuts to your daily meal plan. Eat them as a snack or add them to a smoothie or a salad.

- Drink healthy beverages all day, especially green tea and water.
- Pay attention to fiber. Sources include whole grains, raw produce, nuts and seeds, and beans and legumes.

Focus on Plant-Based Foods

The Mediterranean diet has a plant-forward philosophy, meaning that the majority of your meals should be based around plants, whole grains, and healthy fats, and less on meats, dairy, and eggs. This requires that those who eat a standard American diet change the way they think about the food—in particular, the meat—they consume.

essential

Preparing meals in advance is an easy way to keep on track, and it makes life easier during a busy week. Spend time on the weekend selecting a few recipes to make in advance. Cold salads, soups, and stews are all excellent make-ahead options, and you can divide them into reusable containers for lunches and dinners all week.

When you plan meals on a Mediterranean diet, start the way the locals do—with vegetables. Whole foods (meaning foods that are minimally processed and fresh) are best. When you plan meals around whole, plant-based foods, you eliminate the risk of consuming the added sugar, fat, and salt commonly found in convenience foods. Plan your meals in advance, making a plan for breakfast, lunch, dinner, snacks, and dessert ahead of time so you can reduce your reliance on meat. Make more shopping trips to the grocery store per week to ensure you have the freshest vegetables and fruits on hand for meals.

Eat Seasonally

Fruits and vegetables taste best when they are eaten in season. Become familiar with what produce is fresh and in season where you live, and base your meal plans on those foods. Visit your local farmers' market and talk to the individuals who are selling fresh produce. Ask them what they love and how they like to prepare it. Seasonal fruits and vegetables have more flavor, pack more nutrition, and are generally less expensive, so enjoy the finest fruits and vegetables the season has to offer.

Enjoy Healthy Fats

For cooking and making dressings, olive oil should be your go-to choice, but there are other ways to incorporate healthy fats into your diet. For example, add nuts, olives, avocados, and seeds to grain-based salads or leafy green salads, or incorporate them into dips or dressings. Tahini (sesame paste) can be added to salad dressings to give them richness and a pleasantly nutty flavor. Olives make an excellent snack alone but can also be added to stews, salads, and egg dishes. Get creative in the ways you add healthy fats to your

recipes, and remember to enjoy your fats in moderation.

Eat What You Love

What good is a diet if you don't eat what you crave and enjoy? Above all, cook and eat foods you love. Look for recipes that feature vegetables, fruits, and other plant-based ingredients that you truly enjoy, and find ways to modify recipes with ingredients you may not be as fond of. Explore the market and try new foods, and experiment with fresh herbs and spices. Remember that food is more than a way to nourish your body—it's a way to nourish your soul. Finally, try new things. If there is an ingredient in a recipe you have not used before, why not be adventurous? You won't know what you might like unless you give it a taste. Your new favorite ingredient may be waiting for you to discover it in your local farmers' market.

Stocking a Mediterranean Kitchen

Mediterranean food is flavorful and simple to prepare. Having a well-stocked pantry will make planning and preparing a Mediterranean meal even simpler. Here are some items you should always have on hand so that you are ready to cook many different Mediterranean meals.

Olive Oil

Extra-virgin olive oil is a staple of Mediterranean cooking. Most countries surrounding the Mediterranean Sea produce their own olive oil. Ripe olives are pressed and the oil is filtered and then bottled or canned for consumer use.

Olive oil is used in cooking, baking, and dressings, and for frying. The smoke point for olive oil is 410°F, which is well above the ideal frying temperature of 365°F–375°F, so go ahead and fry with olive oil! Spend some time trying out different kinds to discover which ones you like the most. A good-quality olive oil can make a simple dish outstanding.

Spices and Herbs

Mediterranean cuisine uses a variety of herbs and spices. The recipes in this book feature common Mediterranean herbs such as parsley, dill, rosemary, thyme, sage, mint, fennel fronds, bay leaf, tarragon, lemon verbena, and oregano. Whenever possible, it's best to use herbs in their fresh state. However, oregano is more pungent in its dried state and goes wonderfully with Mediterranean ingredients, so feel free to use dried oregano if you don't have fresh leaves. Herbs are also good for making teas. The most popular ones are chamomile, mint, sage, and lemon verbena.

Spices add warmth to many dishes. Some common Mediterranean spices to keep on hand include cinnamon, cloves, allspice, nutmeg, anise, saffron, crushed red pepper flakes, and mastiha. Mastiha is a spice that comes from the island of Chios, Greece, in the eastern Mediterranean. Mastiha is harvested from the sap of the local *Pistacia lentiscus* tree at specific times in the year. It has a unique woody, slightly piney, and incense-like flavor.

It is traditionally used in Christmas and Easter breads and desserts, but you can use it in savory dishes as well. Buy spices in small amounts as they tend to get stale when stored for too long.

essential

In order to consume fresh, less processed foods, try the following tip: Make a grocery list once a week that always includes fresh foods that have long shelf lives. These foods include apples, oranges, baby carrots, and romaine lettuce. All are readily available and inexpensive, and most people like them.

Dairy Products

Most of the cheese in the Mediterranean region is made from sheep's and goat's milk. These cheeses are easier to digest and have a more complex texture and flavor than the cheeses made from cow's milk that are common in North America. For example, a true feta cheese is made only in Greece, and it is made from sheep's or goat's milk or a blend of the two. Buy feta made in Greece; otherwise, it is not true feta.

Other Greek cheeses referenced in this book are kefalotyri, which is a sharp sheep's milk cheese; graviera, which is similar to a Gruyère; and kasseri, which is a mild table cheese. Halloumi is a wonderful cheese from Cyprus that holds up well on a grill. Romano, Parmesan, ricotta, and mascarpone cheeses are all familiar cheeses from the Mediterranean region.

Greek yogurt is a thick, flavorful yogurt that can be eaten on its own, with fruit, or in recipes as a healthier alternative to sour cream.

Beans and Lentils

The Mediterranean diet is one of the most healthful in the world because it includes a large amount of beans and legumes. Most beans and lentils you purchase in the store are dried, meaning they will keep for a long time in your pantry. Make sure you have plenty of navy beans, butter beans, lentils, and chickpeas. Dried beans require soaking overnight before they can be used, so having canned beans on hand is good for those days when you're in a hurry. Chickpeas and navy beans are good choices.

Whole Grains

Whole grains figure prominently in Mediterranean cooking, and grocers know this. Whole grains like farro, wheat berries, and quinoa have become familiar and are included on many shopping lists. Buy your favorite whole grains and store in a cool, dry place.

Stocks

A good stock will elevate any dish. Making your own stock lets you choose which flavors to add and, most important, how much salt to add. Keep your freezer well "stocked" with quart-sized containers of vegetable stock.

Tomatoes, Potatoes, and Citrus Fruits

Although tomatoes, potatoes, lemons, and oranges are more recent additions to the Mediterranean pantry, it is hard to imagine cooking Mediterranean dishes without them. Buy tomatoes when they are in season. If you must use them in the winter, cherry tomatoes are a good choice. Always have cans of tomato paste and plum tomatoes on hand. They are great for flavoring sauces, soups, and stews.

Citrus fruits are widely available all year, but you can also use preserved lemons, a great pantry staple. Potatoes vary in color, texture, and size. Experiment with different kinds and discover your favorites.

Olives

Have a variety of green and black olives in your pantry. They are wonderful for garnishing salads, making dips, or just eating as a snack.

Vinegars, Honey, and Molasses

Balsamic, red wine, white wine, and cider vinegars are a must in a Mediterranean pantry. They are used to flavor stews, soups, salads, and even desserts. Honey has been a part of Mediterranean cooking for centuries, and it continues to be an essential ingredient in sweet and savory dishes. You will also find sweeteners such as pomegranate molasses and grape molasses in desserts and in dressings for salads.

Kitchen Equipment

Most Mediterranean kitchens aren't full of fancy gadgets—just a few trusty tools can take care of most cooking tasks. Invest in a good chef's knife. Choose one that fits your hand properly and has a good-quality blade. If you invest wisely, this knife will last you a lifetime.

A mortar and pestle is necessary for grinding spices, making pastes, and mixing dips. Don't bother getting a small one. Find a strong, sturdy one that holds at least 3 cups. Avoid ceramic or glass varieties; wood or hard-stone mortars and pestles are the best.

Cheese, vegetables, garlic, and onions can be grated by hand using a box grater. A Microplane grater is indispensable for zesting citrus and grating spices. A food processor is also handy for puréeing and mixing dough. And immersion blenders are an efficient way to blend soups.

Every kitchen should have a meat thermometer and a candy thermometer. The meat thermometer will help you determine when your meat is cooked to a safe temperature. Candy thermometers give you accurate temperatures for frying and making desserts.

Losing Weight with the Green Mediterranean Diet

Weight loss will happen when you change and maintain lifestyle behaviors. The Green Mediterranean diet is a good option for weight loss because it offers a variety of foods; focuses on lower-calorie, higher-fiber plant foods; and recognizes the importance of activity.

> **fact**
>
> Every pound of body weight is equal to 3,500 calories, so when you are trying to lose or gain weight, you must make a change in calories consumed, or burned, equal to that amount. Consuming lower-calorie foods makes it easy to stay full and reduce calories.

Compared to other diets, the Green Mediterranean diet provides most nutrients needed for health, it is high in fiber, the source of fat is of a healthier type, and more of the protein comes from plant foods. It promotes healthy fats, which can aid in satiety, making it easier to follow the diet. At the same time, the fiber content keeps you feeling full longer, so it is easier to space meals further apart. Another aspect of the diet that helps with weight loss is the role of the fluid content of the foods. The fruits and vegetables in the diet provide a lot of water, which will make you feel full.

Unlike other diets that are popular today, the Mediterranean diet has a high carbohydrate content, which helps avoid the triggers for hunger, thus reducing the frequency of binge eating. It's a commonsense diet filled with delicious options, which means you're likelier to follow it for long periods of time.

Add Activity to Promote Weight Loss

Regular physical activity is important to the body for several reasons. Regular activity provides the following benefits:

- Aids weight loss
- Strengthens the heart, lungs, and blood vessels
- Helps improve your mental state
- Can help lower blood triglycerides and cholesterol
- Reduces body fat and preserves muscle
- Helps lower blood pressure
- Lowers blood sugar levels

Regular activity keeps the body working at its peak, which improves your overall quality of life. People who get regular activity find they have more energy to do the things they want to do. Aim for at least two and a half hours of moderate-intensity activity every week, such as walking briskly, taking a group exercise class, or riding a bike. Along with this activity, add some muscle-strengthening activities two or more days a week. Muscle-strengthening activities include lifting weights, working with resistance bands, doing push-ups or sit-ups, or yoga.

This activity should include all parts of the body, so make sure you work your arms, legs, back, chest, shoulders, and abdomen.

If you already include moderate activity in your routine, try adding one hour and fifteen minutes of vigorous activity each week. Vigorous activities include jogging, running, swimming laps, riding a bike uphill, or playing tennis or other sports.

alert

Before you embark on any type of exercise routine, be sure you get a physical and talk with your doctor about your plans for activity. Discuss any regimen you're planning to do to be sure you are fit for it.

Exercise can be a fun by-product of travel. Combining sightseeing with exercise turns it into a joy. Take a walking or biking tour when you visit a new city. Add daily beach walks to a seaside vacation. Break up a long car trip with some hikes along the way. But you don't have to fly off to faraway places…being a tourist in your own town is fun and a good source of exercise.

Easy Mediterranean Cooking at Home

Now that you've learned the basics of Mediterranean cuisine, it's time to experiment in your own kitchen. Refer back to this chapter for tips and guidance as you start your culinary adventures.

The recipes in this book call for fresh ingredients that you can find in any grocery store, and they are broken down into easy-to-follow steps. You'll discover that vibrant, healthful meals don't have to take all day to cook. Most of these dishes can be made in 45 minutes or less. Some need a little time for marinating or slow cooking.

Don't get too hung up on specific ingredients. If you can't find a particular ingredient, substitute something similar. Dried herbs work in place of fresh, canned lentils and beans are great pantry items, and there are many substitution options for olive oil and cheeses…too many to mention! Swap shrimp for chicken breast or replace either with tofu.

In the cold months, all-in-one-pan meals can be made in a skillet, pot, or deep baking dish in your oven. In the summer months, get outdoors and use your grill. The grill offers quick and healthful cooking alternatives, and with a bit of practice, anyone can become a grill master!

Of course, the easiest way to make weeknight dinners is not to cook at all. But you don't have to resort to fast food and takeout. When you have time, make double or triple batches of soups, entrées, and sauces, and then freeze them in meal-sized containers. On those hectic nights when everyone is hungry and no one wants to cook, you'll have a selection of healthful, delicious meals just waiting to be defrosted and reheated.

Creating an Eating Plan

The recipes in this book will provide you with a foundation to create your own version of the Green Mediterranean diet. Do you want to lose weight? Restrict your daily calories to 1,200–1,400 for women or 1,500–1,800 for men; keep your consumption of poultry, seafood, and dairy products to a minimum; and drink a Mankai smoothie once a day.

But if your goal is to move more gradually to a healthier diet, mix and match the recipes to suit your preferences while still focusing on plant-based foods. It's not difficult to add a handful of walnuts to your day. Replace some of the liquids you normally drink with hot or iced green tea. If you're not a fan of Mankai, look for other ways to increase the plant proteins in your diet. Tofu, chickpeas, lentils, flaxseed, chia seeds, quinoa, and nuts are all great options. And don't forget dessert—you don't have to give it up! Allow yourself a treat once in a while. Keep portions reasonable and try to incorporate fruits whenever possible.

The Mediterranean lifestyle is not a short-term diet—it's a way of life. So find some favorite recipes to share with family and friends and remember to slow down and enjoy the meal and the company. Live like the Mediterranean people do and love your food!

CHAPTER 2

Breakfast

Greek Yogurt with Honey and Granola

SERVES 6

Per Serving:

Calories	270
Fat	8g
Sodium	80mg
Carbohydrates	41g
Fiber	3g
Sugar	27g
Protein	10g

Berries and granola add fiber to your breakfast, which will keep you feeling full all morning. Use your favorite store-bought granola for a quicker version.

1 cup rolled oats

¼ cup chopped pecans

¼ cup maple syrup

2 tablespoons packed light brown sugar

1 tablespoon canola oil

⅛ teaspoon salt

1½ cups plain low-fat Greek yogurt

⅓ cup blueberries

⅔ cup raspberries

⅔ cup sliced strawberries

3 tablespoons honey

1 Preheat oven to 300°F. Spray a large baking sheet with nonstick cooking spray.

2 In a large bowl, stir together oats, pecans, maple syrup, sugar, oil, and salt.

3 Spread mixture onto prepared baking sheet. Bake for 1 hour, stirring every 15 minutes. Set aside to cool at least 15 minutes.

4 Divide yogurt among six small bowls and top with granola and berries.

5 Drizzle honey over each bowl and serve.

Fig, Apricot, and Almond Granola

Cardamom is a wonderful, earthy spice that lends a citrusy note to this granola.

⅓ cup vegetable oil

⅓ cup honey

2 tablespoons granulated sugar

1 teaspoon vanilla extract

4 cups old-fashioned oats

1¼ cups sliced almonds

½ cup chopped dried apricots

½ cup chopped dried figs

½ cup packed light brown sugar

½ teaspoon salt

½ teaspoon ground cardamom

1 Preheat oven to 300°F. Lightly spray two large baking sheets with nonstick cooking spray.

2 In a small saucepan over medium heat, add oil, honey, granulated sugar, and vanilla. Cook 5 minutes until sugar is dissolved. Remove pan from heat and cool 2 minutes.

3 In a large bowl, add oats, almonds, apricots, figs, brown sugar, salt, and cardamom. Mix with your hands to combine.

4 Pour honey mixture over oat mixture. Using your hands (if it is too hot, use a wooden spoon), toss ingredients together to make sure everything is well coated. Spread granola evenly on prepared baking sheets. Bake 30 minutes, stirring every 10 minutes.

5 Let granola cool completely on the baking sheets, then break it up into pieces. Store in an airtight container in the pantry up to 3 weeks.

MAKES 6 CUPS

Per Serving (½ cup):

Calories	350
Fat	15g
Sodium	100mg
Carbohydrates	50g
Fiber	6g
Sugar	24g
Protein	8g

DRIED FRUITS

Dried fruits such as figs, raisins, dates, and apricots have been part of the Mediterranean diet for centuries. Drying fruit is one of the oldest forms of preservation and is still popular today.

Baklava Oatmeal

SERVES 4

Per Serving:

Calories	280
Fat	12g
Sodium	10mg
Carbohydrates	39g
Fiber	6g
Sugar	11g
Protein	7g

ABOUT STEEL-CUT OATS

Steel-cut oats are the whole-grain inner parts of the oat kernel that have been cut into pieces. They take longer to cook than traditional rolled oats, so preparing them in the slow cooker is the perfect way to make them for breakfast.

If you've ever enjoyed baklava—the sweet, nutty dessert bars found at many Greek restaurants—you're going to love this simple recipe. Baked with cinnamon and topped with a sweet baklava streusel and a drizzle of honey, this healthful oatmeal is a delicious breakfast choice any morning of the week.

4 cups plus ½ teaspoon water, divided

1 cup steel-cut oats

1½ teaspoons ground cinnamon, divided

½ cup chopped walnuts

1 teaspoon sugar

2 tablespoons honey

1 Spray the bottom of a small (1½- to 3-quart) slow cooker with nonstick cooking spray.

2 Place 4 cups water, oats, and 1 teaspoon cinnamon in slow cooker. Stir until combined. Cover and cook on low for 8 hours.

3 Just before serving, in a large skillet over medium heat, add walnuts. Sprinkle with remaining ½ teaspoon cinnamon, sugar, and remaining ½ teaspoon water. Cook about 3 minutes, just until sugar begins to bubble and walnuts turn a light, toasted golden-brown color.

4 Divide oats among four bowls. Spoon walnut mixture evenly over oatmeal. Drizzle with honey before serving.

Strapatsatha (Scrambled Eggs with Tomatoes)

Strapatsatha is a dish Sephardic Jews brought to Greece from Spain. It's a kind of omelet with fresh tomatoes and feta. There are many variations of this classic dish. If you can, use organic free-range eggs—they taste so much better!

1 tablespoon extra-virgin olive oil

4 large ripe tomatoes, halved and pressed through a box grater

½ cup diced banana pepper

3 scallions, trimmed and sliced

½ cup crumbled feta cheese

8 large eggs, beaten

½ teaspoon ground black pepper

1 Heat oil in a large skillet over medium-high heat and add tomatoes. Cook 5 minutes until most of the liquid is evaporated. Add banana pepper and scallions and cook 2 more minutes. Add feta and cook 1 minute.

2 Add eggs and carefully stir until just set. Sprinkle with black pepper before serving.

SERVES 6

Per Serving:

Calories	180
Fat	12g
Sodium	220mg
Carbohydrates	7g
Fiber	2g
Sugar	4g
Protein	12g

Baked Eggs with Spinach and Cheese

SERVES 4

Per Serving:

Calories	470
Fat	23g
Sodium	790mg
Carbohydrates	40g
Fiber	6g
Sugar	8g
Protein	29g

This is an excellent brunch, lunch, or supper. Everyone loves it. Even better, it's easy to put together during a busy day.

1½ cups corn bread crumbs

3 (10-ounce) packages frozen spinach, thawed and moisture squeezed out

2 tablespoons unsalted butter, melted

½ cup shredded Swiss cheese

½ teaspoon ground nutmeg

½ teaspoon salt

½ teaspoon ground black pepper

1 cup whole milk

8 large eggs

1 Spray a 4- to 5-quart slow cooker with nonstick cooking spray. Sprinkle corn bread crumbs on the bottom of the slow cooker.

2 In a medium bowl, mix spinach, butter, cheese, nutmeg, salt, and pepper together. Stir in milk. Spread mixture on top of corn bread crumbs.

3 Using the back of a tablespoon, make eight depressions in spinach mixture. Break open eggs one at a time and place 1 egg in each hole.

4 Cover and cook on low 3 hours or on high 1½–2 hours until yolks are cooked through but not hard.

Tomato and Goat Cheese Breakfast Casserole

SERVES 6

Per Serving:

Calories	160
Fat	10g
Sodium	350mg
Carbohydrates	6g
Fiber	1g
Sugar	4g
Protein	12g

HERBS AND SPICES

People often confuse herbs with spices. Herbs are green and come from plant leaves. Lavender is the only herb (in Western cooking) that is a flower. Frequently used herbs include parsley, basil, oregano, thyme, rosemary, cilantro, and mint. Spices come from roots, tubers, barks, berries, or seeds. These include black pepper, cinnamon, nutmeg, allspice, cumin, turmeric, ginger, cardamom, and coriander.

Tomatoes and oregano pair elegantly with goat cheese to create a luscious casserole that works just as well for a light dinner as it does for a weekend brunch.

8 large eggs

1 cup low-fat milk

½ teaspoon salt

1 teaspoon ground black pepper

2 cups halved cherry tomatoes

¼ cup chopped fresh oregano

½ cup crumbled goat cheese

1 teaspoon extra-virgin olive oil

1 In a large bowl, whisk together eggs, milk, salt, and pepper until combined. Stir in tomatoes, oregano, and goat cheese; mix well again.

2 Grease a 4- to 5-quart slow cooker with oil.

3 Pour egg mixture into slow cooker and cook on low 4–6 hours or on high 2–3 hours. The casserole is done when a knife inserted into the center comes out clean. Serve hot.

Eggs in Italian Bread

Use the best crusty bread you can find for this classic Italian break-fast. For more fiber, choose a whole-grain loaf.

6 (2") slices crusty Italian bread

3 teaspoons extra-virgin olive oil, divided

2 medium red bell peppers, seeded and thinly sliced

1 small shallot, peeled and minced

6 large eggs

½ teaspoon salt

½ teaspoon ground black pepper

SERVES 6	
Per Serving:	
Calories	160
Fat	8g
Sodium	380mg
Carbohydrates	13g
Fiber	1g
Sugar	3g
Protein	9g

1 Using a cookie cutter or drinking glass, cut out large circles from the center of each bread slice. Discard center pieces and set hollowed-out bread slices aside.

2 Heat 1 teaspoon oil in a medium skillet over medium heat. Sauté bell peppers and shallot 5–7 minutes until tender. Remove from skillet and drain on paper towels; keep warm.

3 Heat remaining 2 teaspoons oil in a large skillet over medium heat. Place bread slices in pan. Crack 1 egg into hollowed-out center of each bread slice. Cook 5 minutes, then flip carefully and cook 3 minutes more. Transfer to plates and top with bell pepper mixture.

4 Season with salt and black pepper before serving.

Mediterranean Omelet

This simple omelet is light and fluffy. It's a quick but sophisticated breakfast. The turkey bacon can be replaced with soy bacon if you like or it can be omitted altogether.

2 large eggs

6 large egg whites

¼ cup plain nonfat Greek yogurt

2 teaspoons extra-virgin olive oil, divided

2 ounces uncooked turkey bacon, roughly chopped

3 ounces Swiss cheese, shredded

¼ cup chopped fresh parsley

½ teaspoon ground black pepper

1. In a medium bowl, beat eggs and egg whites until combined, then whisk in yogurt.
2. Heat 1 teaspoon oil in a small skillet over medium-high heat. Quickly sauté bacon about 2 minutes until crisp, then remove and drain on paper towel.
3. Heat remaining 1 teaspoon oil in a large cast iron skillet or sauté pan over medium heat. Pour in egg mixture, then sprinkle in bacon and cheese. Stir once only. Continuously move the pan, using a spatula to push the edges inward slightly to allow egg mixture to pour outward and solidify. Cook about 5 minutes until mostly firm, then use a spatula to fold omelet in half.
4. Reduce heat to low, cover, and cook 2 minutes more. Sprinkle with parsley and pepper and serve.

SERVES 6

Per Serving:

Calories	160
Fat	10g
Sodium	330mg
Carbohydrates	2g
Fiber	0g
Sugar	1g
Protein	14g

SEASON THE PAN

A properly seasoned cast iron skillet is worth its weight in gold. To season it, generously coat the pan with oil, put it in a warm oven for about an hour, then wipe clean. Avoid using detergents to clean your pan, and always make sure to dry it thoroughly. A thin coat of oil after each use will extend the life of the seasoning. Most importantly, using a cast iron pan often is the best way to keep it seasoned.

Poached Eggs on Greek Yogurt with Koulouri

SERVES 4

Per Serving:

Calories	570
Fat	28g
Sodium	1,180mg
Carbohydrates	51g
Fiber	0g
Sugar	7g
Protein	29g

KOULOURI AND SIMIT

Koulouri are bread rings encrusted with sesame seeds. They're crunchy on the outside with a soft and chewy interior. In Turkey, similar bread rings are called simit. Look for them at Greek or Middle Eastern bakeries. If you can't find either, a small sesame bagel can be substituted.

For a truly authentic Mediterranean breakfast, use goat's or sheep's milk yogurt if you can find it.

4 Greek koulouri (or simit) rings

4 large eggs

4 teaspoons white distilled vinegar

2 cups plain low-fat Greek yogurt, at room temperature

2 tablespoons extra-virgin olive oil

½ teaspoon smoked paprika

1 teaspoon salt

½ teaspoon ground black pepper

4 teaspoons chopped fresh chives

1 Preheat oven to 250°F. Line a plate with paper towels and set aside.

2 Wrap koulouri in foil and place directly on oven rack to warm 15 minutes. Crack eggs into four separate small bowls or ramekins and set aside.

3 Fill a large high-sided skillet with water to a depth of 2". Place over medium heat and bring to a simmer. Stir in vinegar. Carefully tip eggs, one at a time, into the water and reduce heat to low. Cook eggs 3–4 minutes until the whites are set.

4 Use a slotted spoon to transfer eggs to lined plate.

5 Divide yogurt evenly among four plates. Top each plate with a warm koulouri ring. Place a poached egg inside each koulouri ring.

6 In a small bowl, whisk together oil and paprika. Drizzle over eggs.

7 Sprinkle with salt, pepper, and chives. Serve immediately.

Fruit-Stuffed French Toast

The rich, eggy flavor of challah is perfect for this easy special occasion French toast.

½ teaspoon extra-virgin olive oil

1 large loaf challah bread, sliced into 6 (3"-thick) slices

½ cup sliced strawberries

½ cup blueberries

1 cup diced peaches

2 large eggs

4 large egg whites

¼ cup skim milk

1 cup orange juice

¼ cup nonfat plain yogurt

2 tablespoons confectioners' sugar

SERVES 12	
Per Serving:	
Calories	220
Fat	3.5g
Sodium	340mg
Carbohydrates	37g
Fiber	1g
Sugar	9g
Protein	9g

1 Preheat oven to 375°F. Grease a baking sheet with oil.

2 Cut a slit into the bottom crust of each bread slice to form a pocket.

3 In a medium bowl, stir together strawberries, blueberries, and peaches. Fill each bread pocket with about ⅓ cup fruit mixture. Press the pocket closed.

4 In a large shallow bowl, beat eggs, egg whites, and milk until combined. Dip bread slices into egg mixture, letting them fully absorb the mixture. Place bread on prepared baking sheet. Bake 20 minutes, flipping bread halfway through cooking time.

5 While bread is baking, bring orange juice to a boil in a small saucepan over medium-high heat. Cook about 15 minutes until juice is syrupy and reduced by half.

6 Remove French toast from oven and cut each slice in half diagonally. Serve each half with a dollop of yogurt, a drizzle of reduced juice, and a sprinkling of confectioners' sugar.

Breakfast Bruschetta

SERVES 4

Per Serving:

Calories	290
Fat	22g
Sodium	370mg
Carbohydrates	14g
Fiber	1g
Sugar	3g
Protein	10g

TOMATOES

It's hard to imagine Mediterranean cuisine without tomatoes. Their bright flavor and rich color make them a staple ingredient in most dishes. The tomato came to Europe via the explorer Hernán Cortés in the 1500s after he discovered the Aztecs eating them in the New World.

It's not unusual for a Mediterranean breakfast dish to be dominated by vegetables.

4 (¾") slices Italian or French bread

3 tablespoons extra-virgin olive oil, divided

¼ cup pesto

2 large eggs

2 large egg whites

1 medium tomato, cored and diced

½ cup chopped roasted red bell pepper

¼ cup shredded mozzarella cheese

1 teaspoon chopped chives

1 Heat a grill pan over medium-high heat. Brush both sides of bread slices with 2 tablespoons oil and grill about 3 minutes per side until lightly browned.

2 Place toasted bread on a baking sheet and spread with pesto.

3 Preheat broiler. In a medium bowl, lightly beat eggs and egg whites. Stir in tomato.

4 Heat remaining 1 tablespoon oil in a medium skillet over medium heat. Add egg mixture and stir once. Continuously move the pan, using a spatula to push the edges inward slightly to allow egg mixture to pour outward and solidify. Cook about 6 minutes until mixture is firm, then use a spatula to fold eggs in half.

5 Remove from pan and cut into four pieces. Place on top of bread slices and top with roasted pepper and mozzarella. Broil about 2 minutes until cheese melts. Sprinkle with chives and serve immediately.

Multigrain Cornmeal Waffles

SERVES 4

Per Serving:

Calories	300
Fat	18g
Sodium	500mg
Carbohydrates	30g
Fiber	4g
Sugar	7g
Protein	7g

Serve these slightly crunchy waffles with fresh berries or diced apples and cinnamon.

½ **cup fine cornmeal**

½ **cup whole-wheat flour**

1 **tablespoon ground chia seed**

½ **teaspoon salt**

½ **teaspoon baking soda**

1 **teaspoon baking powder**

1 **cup low-fat milk**

1 **teaspoon vanilla extract**

1 **large egg**

¼ **cup sunflower oil**

1 **tablespoon honey**

1 Spray a waffle maker with nonstick cooking spray and preheat.

2 In a small bowl, place cornmeal, flour, chia seed, salt, baking soda, and baking powder and stir with a fork.

3 In a separate medium bowl, whisk together milk, vanilla, egg, oil, and honey. Slowly whisk in cornmeal mixture until incorporated.

4 Ladle about ¼ cup batter into the center of the waffle maker. Close and cook according to manufacturer's instructions. Remove waffle and repeat with remaining batter.

5 Serve warm.

Banana-Walnut Bread

This moist, delicious bread is so good, you'll want to buy extra bananas just so you can make it. The longer they ripen, the better!

2 cups all-purpose flour

1 teaspoon baking soda

2 teaspoons baking powder

¼ teaspoon salt

3 large ripe bananas, peeled and mashed

¼ cup low-fat buttermilk

½ cup unsalted butter, softened

½ cup granulated sugar

½ cup packed light brown sugar

1 teaspoon vanilla extract

2 large eggs

½ cup chopped walnuts

1 medium firm banana, peeled and cut in half lengthwise

SERVES 10

Per Serving:

Calories	350
Fat	14g
Sodium	210mg
Carbohydrates	53g
Fiber	3g
Sugar	27g
Protein	5g

1 Preheat oven to 350°F. Line the bottom and sides of a 9" × 4.5" loaf pan with parchment paper, allowing a couple of inches overhang on either side.

2 In a medium bowl, combine flour, baking soda, baking powder, and salt. In a separate small bowl, using a fork, mix mashed bananas and buttermilk.

3 In a separate large bowl, place butter, granulated sugar, brown sugar, and vanilla. Using a handheld electric mixer, blend 2–3 minutes until smooth. Add eggs one at a time, beating after each addition.

4 While mixing, slowly add flour mixture and beat just until combined. Stir in banana mixture and walnuts with a rubber spatula.

5 Pour batter into prepared loaf pan. Top with banana halves, cut side up.

6 Bake 50–60 minutes until a toothpick inserted into the center of the bread comes out clean.

7 Cool in pan 5 minutes, then carefully use the parchment paper to lift banana bread out of the pan. Cool completely on a wire rack at least 1 hour before serving.

Blueberry Corn Bread Muffins

There's no need to choose between blueberry and corn muffins. A handful of blueberries provide bursts of sweetness as well as fiber, vitamin C, and antioxidants.

1 cup all-purpose flour

¾ cup cornmeal

2 tablespoons baking powder

1 teaspoon salt

⅔ cup low-fat milk

⅓ cup unsalted butter, melted

¾ cup sugar

1 large egg

1 cup fresh or frozen blueberries

1 Preheat oven to 425°F. Line a twelve-cup muffin tin with paper liners.

2 In a medium bowl, using a fork, stir together flour, cornmeal, baking powder, and salt.

3 In a large bowl, whisk together milk, butter, and sugar. Whisk in egg until combined. Stir in flour mixture just until incorporated. Fold in blueberries.

4 Pour batter into muffin tin, filling each cup three-quarters full. Bake 20 minutes until a toothpick inserted into the center of a muffin comes out clean.

5 Cool in the tin 5 minutes, then remove muffins from the tin and cool on a wire rack at least 15 minutes. Serve warm or at room temperature.

CHAPTER 3

Snacks and Smoothies

Mankai Protein Shake

SERVES 1

Per Serving:

Calories	360
Fat	4g
Sodium	110mg
Carbohydrates	74g
Fiber	6g
Sugar	25g
Protein	14g

FROZEN FRUIT IS GREAT FOR SMOOTHIES

Keep a stash of fruits for smoothies in your freezer. Prepare them first: Remove peels, pits, seeds, or cores, then cut them into bite-sized pieces. Place fruit pieces on a parchment-lined baking sheet and freeze until solid. Transfer the frozen fruit to zip-top plastic bags, and you'll always be ready for a smoothie.

Mankai, or duckweed, is a tiny plant with a giant nutritional profile. A serving provides as much iron as 6 cups of spinach, as much complete protein as an egg, and as much vitamin A as a cup of red bell pepper. Frozen cubes are available online at EatMankai.com. It's also sold in a powdered version at vitamin and supplement stores.

3 frozen Mankai cubes (85g)

1 cup baby spinach leaves

1½ cups diced frozen pineapple

½ medium frozen banana, peeled and chopped

2 teaspoons honey

½ cup unsweetened almond milk

1 tablespoon grated fresh ginger

1 Place all ingredients in a blender. Begin blending on low speed, then increase to high and process about 2 minutes until smooth.

2 Pour into a tall glass and serve.

Blueberry-Flax Smoothie

Flaxseed is a nutritious alternative to Mankai duckweed. Consuming ground flaxseed in smoothies, sauces, and snacks can help to lower blood pressure and "bad" cholesterol levels.

1 teaspoon ground flaxseed

1 cup unsweetened almond milk

¼ cup fresh or frozen blueberries

1 teaspoon honey

1 tablespoon chopped fresh mint

1 Place all ingredients in a blender. Begin blending on low speed, then increase to high and process about 2 minutes until smooth.

2 Pour into a tall glass and serve.

SERVES 1

Per Serving:

Calories	110
Fat	4.5g
Sodium	135mg
Carbohydrates	16g
Fiber	2g
Sugar	11g
Protein	2g

Mango-Ginger Green Smoothie

You can freeze ginger in tablespoon amounts. First peel and grate it, then scoop it onto a parchment-lined baking sheet. Freeze until firm, and then transfer to a zip-top plastic bag. It will keep about 6 months.

1½ cups apple juice

1 tablespoon grated fresh ginger

1 cup chopped frozen mango

2 cups baby spinach

1   Place all ingredients in a blender. Begin blending on low speed, then increase to high and process about 2 minutes until smooth.

2   Pour into two tall glasses and serve.

SERVES 2

Per Serving:

Calories	170
Fat	0g
Sodium	60mg
Carbohydrates	41g
Fiber	3g
Sugar	37g
Protein	2g

Kalimera (Good Morning) Green Smoothie

SERVES 2

Per Serving:

Calories	150
Fat	3.5g
Sodium	110mg
Carbohydrates	30g
Fiber	5g
Sugar	16g
Protein	3g

Kale is a nutrient-dense superfood and an excellent source of vitamin C and beta-carotene. A cup of kale also contains seven times the RDA for vitamin K. Drinking kale juice or eating steamed kale regularly can reduce the amount of cholesterol in the body.

1½ cups unsweetened almond milk

2 cups chopped kale

1 medium frozen banana, peeled and sliced

1 cup diced kiwi

1 Place almond milk and kale in a blender. Begin blending on low speed, then increase to high and process about 2 minutes until smooth.

2 Add banana and kiwi and blend on high speed 1 minute.

3 Pour into two tall glasses and serve.

Tropical Green Smoothie

If you worry about getting enough iron when you're not eating meat, the solution is simple: Eat more spinach! Here's a delicious way to add spinach to your diet.

1½ cups unsweetened coconut water

2 cups baby spinach

½ cup chopped frozen pineapple

½ cup chopped frozen mango

1 medium banana, peeled

1 Place coconut water and spinach in a blender. Begin blending on low speed, then increase to high and process about 2 minutes until smooth.
2 Add pineapple, mango, and banana and blend on high speed 1 minute.
3 Pour into two tall glasses and serve.

SERVES 2

Per Serving:

Calories	150
Fat	0g
Sodium	90mg
Carbohydrates	37g
Fiber	4g
Sugar	22g
Protein	3g

Piña Colada Smoothie

SERVES 2

Per Serving:

Calories	190
Fat	11g
Sodium	60mg
Carbohydrates	24g
Fiber	3g
Sugar	7g
Protein	2g

PACKED WITH VITAMINS AND MINERALS

Pineapple is rich in vitamin C and manganese, and it aids in the absorption of iron in the body.

Add a little vacation happy hour flavor to your breakfast with this delicious healthy frozen drink.

1½ cups canned light coconut milk

1 cup chopped frozen pineapple

2 tablespoons ground flaxseed

1   Place all ingredients in a blender. Begin blending on low speed, then increase to high and process about 2 minutes until smooth.

2   Pour into two tall glasses and serve.

Strawberry-Kiwi Smoothie

Make this sweet and fruity smoothie extra creamy by freezing the chunks of kiwi first.

1½ cups apple juice

1 cup frozen strawberries

4 medium kiwis, peeled and chopped

3 (85g) frozen Mankai cubes

1 Place apple juice and strawberries in a blender. Begin blending on low speed, then increase to high and process about 2 minutes until smooth.

2 Add kiwis and Mankai and blend on high speed 1 minute.

3 Pour into two tall glasses and serve.

SERVES 2

Per Serving:

Calories	240
Fat	2g
Sodium	35mg
Carbohydrates	53g
Fiber	6g
Sugar	38g
Protein	8g

HOW TO PEEL A KIWI

Kiwis are easy to peel with a spoon: Slice the top off the fruit, then insert a teaspoon between the skin and flesh. Rotate the kiwi until all the skin has been separated. Squeeze the skin to pop out a perfectly peeled kiwi.

Mandarin Sunshine Smoothie

SERVES 2

Per Serving:

Calories	170
Fat	3g
Sodium	105mg
Carbohydrates	35g
Fiber	4g
Sugar	19g
Protein	3g

Turmeric can help to increase your body's antioxidant capacity and reduce inflammation. And it adds the sunniest yellow color to this energizing morning smoothie!

1½ cups unsweetened almond milk

1 cup chopped frozen pineapple

4 small mandarin oranges, chilled and peeled

¼ teaspoon ground turmeric

1 Place almond milk and pineapple in a blender. Begin blending on low speed, then increase to high and process about 2 minutes until smooth.

2 Add mandarins and turmeric and blend on high speed 1 minute.

3 Pour into two tall glasses and serve.

Very Berry Green Smoothie

Add a few ice cubes for a slushier texture that's perfect for a summer snack.

1½ cups unsweetened pomegranate juice
½ cup baby spinach
2 tablespoons chopped fresh mint
2 cups frozen mixed berries

1. Place pomegranate juice, spinach, and mint in a blender. Begin blending on low speed, then increase to high and process about 2 minutes until smooth.
2. Add berries and blend on high speed 1 minute.
3. Pour into two tall glasses and serve.

SERVES 2

Per Serving:

Calories	230
Fat	1.5g
Sodium	35mg
Carbohydrates	54g
Fiber	9g
Sugar	38g
Protein	2g

THAT'S A BIG BERRY!

Because they come from a single flower and contain lots of seeds, pomegranates are botanically considered berries. So are bananas, eggplants, and cucumbers.

Olive and Red Pepper Dip

Serve this lovely dip with flatbread or toasted whole-wheat pitas.

SERVES 8

Per Serving:

Calories	160
Fat	17g
Sodium	220mg
Carbohydrates	4g
Fiber	1g
Sugar	1g
Protein	1g

LITTLE DIPPERS

Slice a whole-grain baguette into 1/8" slices. Brush lightly with olive oil and sprinkle with dried tarragon and rosemary. Bake at 350°F 10 minutes until crisp.

½ cup pitted green olives

1 large Roasted Red Pepper (see recipe in Chapter 11), roughly chopped

1 teaspoon balsamic vinegar

⅔ cup soft bread crumbs

2 cloves garlic, peeled and smashed

½ teaspoon crushed red pepper flakes

⅓ cup extra-virgin olive oil

1 In a food processor, combine all ingredients except oil. Pulse to combine but leave the mixture chunky.

2 With the processor running, slowly add oil until completely incorporated. Transfer to a bowl. Refrigerate until cold or serve at room temperature.

Santorini Fava (Yellow Split Pea Dip)

MAKES 3 CUPS

**Per Serving
(2 tablespoons):**

Calories	30
Fat	1.5g
Sodium	35mg
Carbohydrates	3g
Fiber	1g
Sugar	0g
Protein	1g

SPLIT PEAS

Split peas are very high in dietary fiber and protein. They are an excellent and healthful alternative to meat proteins. Unlike other dried beans, you don't need to presoak them before cooking. Just give them a rinse and pick out any shriveled or broken beans, stones, or debris, and they are ready to cook.

In the Greek food sense, fava *has nothing to do with fava beans. Rather, it's a dip made from split peas. Serve it with raw vegetables or whole-grain crackers.*

1 cup yellow split peas

1 small yellow onion, peeled and chopped

1 bay leaf

4 cups water

6 oil-packed sun-dried tomato halves, drained

2 tablespoons red wine vinegar

3 large cloves garlic, peeled

2 small shallots, peeled and chopped

1½ teaspoons dried oregano

½ teaspoon fresh thyme leaves

¼ cup plus 1 tablespoon extra-virgin olive oil, divided

½ teaspoon salt

¼ teaspoon ground black pepper

2 tablespoons drained capers

2 tablespoons chopped red onion

1 In a large saucepan over medium-high heat, combine split peas, yellow onion, bay leaf, and water. Bring to a boil, then reduce heat to medium-low and simmer about 25 minutes until peas are tender. Drain mixture and discard bay leaf.

2 In a food processor, place tomatoes, vinegar, garlic, shallots, oregano, and thyme. Pulse until minced. Add split pea mixture and pulse until combined.

3 With the processor running, slowly pour in ¼ cup oil and process until a smooth paste forms. Add salt and pepper.

4 Transfer mixture to a small bowl or plate. Drizzle with remaining 1 tablespoon oil and garnish with capers and red onion. Serve immediately.

Spinach Dip

Serve this delicious and healthy version of spinach dip with raw vegetables or toasted whole-wheat pita chips.

4 cups baby spinach

1 clove garlic, peeled and minced

⅔ cup walnut halves

1 (14-ounce) can artichoke hearts, drained

1 (4-ounce) jar roasted red peppers, drained and diced

½ cup plain low-fat Greek yogurt

¼ teaspoon salt

½ cup grated Parmesan cheese

1 Preheat oven to 400°F.

2 In a food processor, place spinach, garlic, and walnuts and pulse until finely chopped. Add artichokes and pulse briefly.

3 Transfer mixture to a medium bowl and stir in roasted peppers, yogurt, and salt. Pour into an 8" × 8" baking dish. Top with Parmesan.

4 Bake 15 minutes until cheese melts. Cool 5 minutes before serving.

MAKES 3 CUPS

Per Serving (2 tablespoons):

Calories	30
Fat	1.5g
Sodium	90mg
Carbohydrates	2g
Fiber	1g
Sugar	0g
Protein	2g

FREEZER FRESH

Store walnuts and other nuts in the freezer to extend their shelf life and prevent them from going rancid. There's no need to defrost them before using.

Zesty Bean Dip

Per Serving (2 tablespoons):

Calories	40
Fat	1.5g
Sodium	40mg
Carbohydrates	4g
Fiber	2g
Sugar	0g
Protein	2g

Cannellini are sometimes called white kidney beans or fazolia. You can use navy beans or great northern beans as well for this dip. Serve it with a variety of crisp raw vegetables for a filling and healthy snack.

1 (15-ounce) can cannellini beans, drained and rinsed

2 cloves garlic, peeled and minced

2 tablespoons extra-virgin olive oil

2 tablespoons lemon juice

1 tablespoon grated lemon zest

½ teaspoon fresh thyme leaves

1 teaspoon crushed red pepper flakes

2 tablespoons finely chopped fresh parsley

1 In a medium bowl, place beans and garlic. Mash with a fork until combined but still chunky.

2 Stir in oil, lemon juice, lemon zest, thyme, and red pepper flakes.

3 Transfer to a small serving bowl, top with parsley, and serve.

Hummus

Chickpeas are full of protein and zinc, and they are low in fat. They make this dish both tasty and healthful.

2 cups drained and rinsed canned chickpeas

4 cloves garlic, peeled and smashed

2 scallions, trimmed and chopped

1 large Roasted Red Pepper (see recipe in Chapter 11)

½ cup tahini

2 tablespoons lemon juice

¼ teaspoon crushed red pepper flakes

½ cup extra-virgin olive oil

1 teaspoon salt

1 teaspoon paprika

1 In a food processor, add chickpeas, garlic, scallions, Roasted Red Pepper, tahini, lemon juice, and red pepper flakes. Process until smooth.

2 With the processor running, slowly add oil until completely incorporated. Season with salt. Transfer to a bowl and sprinkle with paprika. Refrigerate until cold or serve at room temperature.

SERVES 12

Per Serving:

Calories	90
Fat	7g
Sodium	125mg
Carbohydrates	4g
Fiber	1g
Sugar	1g
Protein	2g

PAPRIKA

Paprika is made from grinding dried red peppers. Hummus recipes typically call for regular (sweet) paprika, but you could also use hot or smoked paprika for a different flavor.

Pasteli (Honey-Sesame Bars)

These delicious sesame bars contain healthy fats, protein, fiber, and antioxidants—they're the original energy snack. Choose a good-quality honey for these bars.

1½ cups honey

1½ cups toasted sesame seeds

½ cup roughly chopped roasted unsalted almonds

1 tablespoon grated orange zest

¼ teaspoon ground cinnamon

1 Line a baking sheet with parchment paper and set aside.

2 Pour honey into a medium saucepan and clip a candy thermometer to the side of the pan. Heat over medium heat until the temperature reaches 250°F.

3 Add sesame seeds, almonds, orange zest, and cinnamon. Cook and stir another 3 minutes.

4 Pour the mixture onto prepared baking sheet and lay another piece of parchment paper on top.

5 Use a rolling pin to roll out the mixture to ¼" thickness. Remove the top sheet of parchment and allow about 30 minutes to cool completely.

6 Cut into square or diamond shapes and serve. Store in an airtight container with parchment paper placed between layers up to 1 week.

MAKES 20 PIECES

Per Serving (1 piece):

Calories	170
Fat	8g
Sodium	15mg
Carbohydrates	23g
Fiber	2g
Sugar	21g
Protein	4g

TOASTING SESAME SEEDS

Toasting sesame seeds is easy, but it requires some patience. In a dry skillet over medium heat, stir sesame seeds constantly with a wooden spoon until they are toasted to your liking. Toasting can take up to 10 minutes, so be patient. Don't walk away from the pan, because the seeds can burn very quickly.

Halva Energy Balls

MAKES 12 ENERGY BALLS

Per Serving (1 energy ball):

Calories	270
Fat	16g
Sodium	55mg
Carbohydrates	28g
Fiber	3g
Sugar	13g
Protein	6g

Halva is a nutty, soft, and sweet confection found in many Middle Eastern stores. Made from sesame paste, it has a fudge-like consistency. It's usually sold in 8-ounce or 1-pound blocks.

1 cup pitted Medjool dates

½ cup chopped almonds

½ cup chopped walnuts

2 tablespoons light olive oil

8 ounces sesame halva, crumbled

1 cup toasted sesame seeds

1 Line a baking sheet with parchment paper and set aside.

2 Place dates in a medium bowl and cover with room-temperature water. Set aside 15 minutes to soak.

3 Drain dates and place in a food processor with almonds, walnuts, and oil. Pulse until smooth. Transfer to a medium bowl. Stir in halva.

4 Pour sesame seeds onto a large plate. Roll date mixture into 12 balls and roll each ball in sesame seeds until thoroughly coated. Place balls on prepared baking sheet.

5 Transfer baking sheet to freezer and freeze 1 hour. Remove from freezer and transfer balls to a covered plastic container. Refrigerate up to 1 week or freeze up to 1 month.

6 Thaw frozen energy balls 10 minutes before serving.

Walnut-Stuffed Figs

These figs are extraordinary and easy to make, and they look fabulous on a holiday treats platter.

½ cup honey

1 teaspoon ground star anise

⅓ cup fine almond flour

2 tablespoons unsweetened cocoa powder

⅓ cup crushed petit beurre biscuits

1¾ cups ground walnuts, divided

20 dried Greek or Turkish figs

20 walnut halves

1 Heat honey in a medium saucepan over low heat for 5 minutes. Remove from heat and stir in star anise, flour, and cocoa.

2 Transfer mixture to a medium bowl. Add biscuits and 1¼ cups ground walnuts. Stir to combine into a dough, then cover and refrigerate 2 hours.

3 Meanwhile, snip the stems from figs and discard. Gently open the top of each fig with your finger and insert a walnut half into each fig.

4 Line a baking sheet or platter with parchment paper. Pour remaining ½ cup ground walnuts onto a small plate.

5 Remove honey mixture from the refrigerator. Rub your hands with a little vegetable oil, then scoop a heaping tablespoon of the mixture and place it in one hand. Flatten the dough with your other hand, then place a stuffed fig on top. Wrap the fig completely in the dough and roll it in the ground walnuts. Place it on prepared baking sheet or platter. Repeat with remaining ingredients.

6 Cover loosely with foil and freeze overnight. To serve, remove from the freezer, carefully slice each stuffed fig in half, and place in decorative paper cups.

SERVES 20

Per Serving:

Calories	120
Fat	7g
Sodium	10mg
Carbohydrates	15g
Fiber	2g
Sugar	12g
Protein	2g

PETIT BEURRE BISCUITS

Petit beurre biscuits can be found in the international section of the grocery store—look for LU brand from France. If you can't find them, you can substitute Nabisco Social Tea Biscuits.

CHAPTER 4
Easy Lunches

Greek Village Salad

SERVES 6

Per Serving:

Calories	260
Fat	22g
Sodium	640mg
Carbohydrates	9g
Fiber	2g
Sugar	4g
Protein	6g

An authentic Greek salad contains no lettuce of any kind. Use your best olive oil for this salad. You don't need any vinegar; the tomatoes' acidity is enough.

4 medium ripe tomatoes, cored and cut into wedges

½ medium English cucumber, halved and sliced into ½" slices

1 medium green Cubanelle pepper, seeded and sliced

1 small red onion, peeled and thinly sliced

½ teaspoon salt

⅓ cup extra-virgin olive oil

1½ cups cubed feta cheese

8 kalamata olives

1 teaspoon dried oregano

1 Arrange tomatoes and cucumber on a serving plate. Next add pepper and onion. Season vegetables with salt.

2 Drizzle oil over vegetables. Top with feta and olives and sprinkle with oregano.

3 Serve at room temperature.

Chickpea Salad with Roasted Red Peppers and Green Beans

Try using a combination of red, green, yellow, and orange peppers for a more colorful salad.

3 cloves garlic, peeled and minced

1 teaspoon Dijon mustard

2 tablespoons red wine vinegar

¾ teaspoon salt, divided

½ teaspoon ground black pepper, divided

½ cup extra-virgin olive oil

1 (15-ounce) can chickpeas, drained and rinsed

1 pound green beans, trimmed and blanched 5 minutes

2 large Roasted Red Peppers (see recipe in Chapter 11), sliced

1 cup halved pickled cauliflower florets

5 ounces spring mix salad greens

¼ cup chopped fresh parsley

2 teaspoons dried oregano

12 pitted kalamata olives

1 In a large bowl, whisk together garlic, mustard, vinegar, ½ teaspoon salt, and ¼ teaspoon black pepper. Slowly whisk in oil until it is well incorporated.

2 Add chickpeas, green beans, Roasted Red Peppers, and cauliflower. Toss to coat.

3 Add greens, parsley, oregano, olives, and remaining ¼ teaspoon each salt and black pepper. Toss to combine the ingredients and serve immediately.

SERVES 6

Per Serving:

Calories	370
Fat	25g
Sodium	730mg
Carbohydrates	30g
Fiber	8g
Sugar	9g
Protein	8g

KALAMATA OLIVES

Kalamata is a region in Greece that is famous for its olives and its olive oil. Kalamata olives have a distinct brown-green color and are briny and meaty.

Mani-Style Salad

SERVES 4

Per Serving:

Calories	210
Fat	12g
Sodium	820mg
Carbohydrates	24g
Fiber	3g
Sugar	7g
Protein	2g

A "GOOD" FAT

Olive oil, a monounsaturated fat, has been shown to raise HDL levels ("good" cholesterol) in blood.

The Mani region is located in the southernmost tip of the Peloponnese. The rugged land there is rich with citrus and olive groves. This traditional salad dances between sweet and savory: Sweet oranges contrast with briny olives and savory red onion. Extra-virgin olive oil brings all the flavors together.

2 medium Yukon Gold potatoes

3½ teaspoons salt, divided

2 medium navel oranges, peeled and sliced into rounds

½ cup thinly sliced red onion

¾ cup pitted kalamata olives

2 tablespoons extra-virgin olive oil

⅛ teaspoon ground black pepper

1 Place potatoes and 3 teaspoons salt in a medium saucepan. Add enough water to cover and bring to a boil over high heat. Reduce heat to medium-low and simmer 15–20 minutes until tender.

2 Drain potatoes and set aside to cool 30 minutes. Peel cooled potatoes and cut them into ¼" slices.

3 Arrange potato slices on a large plate and sprinkle with ¼ teaspoon salt. Place orange slices on top, followed by onion slices. Scatter olives over the top of the salad.

4 Drizzle with oil and sprinkle with pepper and remaining ¼ teaspoon salt. Serve immediately.

Greek Pita

SERVES 6

Per Serving:

Calories	300
Fat	7g
Sodium	520mg
Carbohydrates	48g
Fiber	2g
Sugar	4g
Protein	10g

Serve these flavorful sandwiches with a green salad for a hearty lunch.

6 (6½") pita rounds

2 medium cucumbers, peeled and diced

1 large red onion, peeled and thinly sliced

¼ cup chopped fresh oregano

½ cup crumbled feta cheese

1 tablespoon extra-virgin olive oil

½ teaspoon ground black pepper

1 Cut a horizontal slit in each pita and stuff with cucumber, onion, oregano, and feta.

2 Drizzle with oil and sprinkle with pepper.

Hummus Power Bowl

Power bowls are filling, nutritious, and tasty. Build one in a large shallow bowl for an at-home lunch, or pack it in a container to take with you for an easy on-the-go meal.

¼ cup hummus

1 cup spring mix salad greens

½ cup drained and rinsed canned chickpeas

¼ cup cooked couscous

½ cup halved cherry tomatoes

½ cup diced English cucumber

½ cup sliced yellow bell pepper

2 tablespoons chopped kalamata olives

1 tablespoon extra-virgin olive oil

1½ teaspoons lemon juice

⅛ teaspoon salt

⅛ teaspoon paprika

1 tablespoon chopped fresh mint

1 Spoon hummus into the center of a wide, shallow bowl. Surround with greens, then top with chickpeas, couscous, tomatoes, cucumber, bell pepper, and olives.

2 In a small bowl, whisk together oil, lemon juice, salt, paprika, and mint. Drizzle over the bowl and serve immediately.

SERVES 1

Per Serving:

Calories	510
Fat	29g
Sodium	1,170mg
Carbohydrates	51g
Fiber	8g
Sugar	10g
Protein	15g

LOTS OF INGREDIENTS; LITTLE EFFORT

Power bowls may have long lists of ingredients, but don't be intimidated. There's minimal preparation involved—just pile the ingredients in a bowl and whisk up a quick dressing to pour over the top.

Lentil Halloumi Bowl

SERVES 1

Per Serving:

Calories	450
Fat	34g
Sodium	870mg
Carbohydrates	25g
Fiber	4g
Sugar	5g
Protein	13g

HALLOUMI

Halloumi is a firm, brined Cypriot cheese that is traditionally made with sheep's or goat's milk, or sometimes a combination of the two. You can find cow's milk halloumi, but it's worth it to search for the real thing from Cyprus. It has a high melting point, so it can handle searing and grilling without falling apart.

Canned lentils are a versatile pantry staple, and they're loaded with fiber and protein. It's a good idea to drain and rinse canned lentils and other legumes to reduce the amount of sodium in your meal.

¼ cup drained and rinsed canned brown lentils

1 cup spring mix salad greens

¼ cup drained and rinsed canned chickpeas

½ cup halved cherry tomatoes

¼ cup diced English cucumber

2 tablespoons chopped kalamata olives

1 teaspoon plus 1 tablespoon extra-virgin olive oil, divided

1 (1-ounce) slice halloumi cheese

1 teaspoon red wine vinegar

2 tablespoons chopped red onion

¼ teaspoon dried oregano

1 Spoon lentils into the center of a wide, shallow bowl. Surround with greens, then top with chickpeas, tomatoes, cucumber, and olives.

2 In a small nonstick skillet over medium-high heat, heat 1 teaspoon oil. Sear halloumi about 1 minute per side until golden brown. Remove from the skillet and add to bowl.

3 In a small bowl, whisk together remaining 1 tablespoon oil, vinegar, onion, and oregano. Spoon over the bowl and serve immediately.

Greek Lentil Power Bowl

Here's a power bowl version of a Greek salad, with lentils and brown rice to add iron and fiber.

½ cup drained and rinsed canned brown or green lentils

½ cup cooked brown rice

½ cup halved cherry tomatoes

¼ cup diced English cucumber

¼ cup diced green bell pepper

¼ cup sliced red onion

¼ cup crumbled feta cheese

¼ cup pitted kalamata olives

2 tablespoons extra-virgin olive oil

1 teaspoon lemon juice

½ teaspoon dried oregano

1 Spoon lentils into the center of two wide, shallow bowls. Surround with rice, then top with tomatoes, cucumber, bell pepper, onion, feta, and olives.

2 In a small bowl, whisk together oil, lemon juice, and oregano. Drizzle over the bowls and serve immediately.

SERVES 2

Per Serving:

Calories	355
Fat	24g
Sodium	560mg
Carbohydrates	29g
Fiber	2g
Sugar	4g
Protein	8g

Artichokes à la Polita

"À la polita" is how Greeks refer to dishes with origins in Constantinople (now Istanbul). This version is popular in springtime.

¼ cup extra-virgin olive oil

2 medium yellow onions, peeled and sliced

4 medium red potatoes, peeled and cut into thirds

3 large carrots, peeled and cut into 2" pieces

1 tablespoon tomato paste

12 medium artichokes, outer layers peeled, trimmed, halved, and chokes removed

1 teaspoon salt

¾ teaspoon ground black pepper

1 cup thawed frozen or fresh peas

½ cup chopped fresh dill

1 large lemon, cut into wedges

1 Heat oil in a large pot over medium-high heat. Stir in onions, potatoes, and carrots. Reduce heat to medium and cover. Simmer 15 minutes.

2 Add tomato paste, artichokes, salt, pepper, and enough water to cover. Bring to a boil over high heat, cover pot, and reduce heat to medium. Cook 10 minutes until artichokes are tender.

3 Gently stir in peas and dill. Remove pot from heat and allow peas to cook in the hot liquid for 5 minutes. Serve hot with lemon wedges.

SERVES 8

Per Serving:

Calories	290
Fat	8g
Sodium	570mg
Carbohydrates	52g
Fiber	16g
Sugar	8g
Protein	12g

EASY ARTICHOKES

If you love artichokes but hate trimming them, look for frozen artichokes in your grocer's freezer. All the work has already been done for you.

Avocado Carpaccio with Shrimp

SERVES 2

Per Serving:

Calories	490
Fat	30g
Sodium	790mg
Carbohydrates	10g
Fiber	8g
Sugar	2g
Protein	47g

EASY BABY SHRIMP

Small cooked baby shrimp can be found in the freezer section at your local supermarket. Defrost them overnight in the refrigerator, give them a quick rinse, and pat them dry with paper towels.

When buying avocados, choose a mix of avocados—some ripe, some a few days from ripening, and a couple that are firm and will need a week before they're ready. This way you won't have to eat them all in one day!

2 cups loosely packed baby arugula

12 ounces cooked small shrimp

1 medium ripe avocado, peeled, pitted, and thinly sliced

1 tablespoon plain low-fat Greek yogurt

1 tablespoon lemon juice

2 tablespoons extra-virgin olive oil

¼ teaspoon salt

¼ teaspoon ground black pepper

1 tablespoon chopped fresh tarragon

2 tablespoons chopped fresh chives

1 On a platter, arrange arugula and top with shrimp and avocado.
2 In a small bowl, whisk together yogurt, lemon juice, oil, salt, pepper, and tarragon. If the dressing is too thick, add a teaspoon or two of water.
3 Spoon dressing over salad and sprinkle with chives. Serve immediately.

Okra in Tomato Sauce

Okra contains mucilage, a syrupy substance that helps to thicken a stew like gumbo or this one. Using frozen baby okra saves time and effort. All you need to do is open the bag and toss them in. You don't even need to defrost them first.

2 tablespoons extra-virgin olive oil

2 medium yellow onions, peeled and sliced

1½ pounds fresh or frozen okra, trimmed

½ cup canned plum tomatoes, hand-crushed

½ cup chopped fresh parsley

3 cloves garlic, peeled and sliced

6 whole allspice berries

2 cups vegetable stock

2 large russet potatoes, peeled and cut into large chunks

½ teaspoon salt

¼ teaspoon ground black pepper

SERVES 6

Per Serving:

Calories	200
Fat	5g
Sodium	330mg
Carbohydrates	37g
Fiber	6g
Sugar	6g
Protein	5g

1 Heat oil in a large saucepan or Dutch oven over medium-high heat. Add onions and sauté 3 minutes. Cover, reduce heat to medium, and simmer 10 minutes.

2 Add okra, tomatoes, parsley, garlic, allspice berries, and stock. Increase heat to high and bring to a boil.

3 Cover, reduce heat to medium-low, and simmer 15 minutes. Add potatoes and simmer 20–25 minutes until fork-tender. Stir in salt and pepper and serve.

Cretan Dakos

SERVES 4

Per Serving:

Calories	300
Fat	14g
Sodium	290mg
Carbohydrates	32g
Fiber	1g
Sugar	5g
Protein	9g

Dakos, or rusks, are hard, twice-baked slices of bread. They're sold at Greek or Middle Eastern grocers. If you can't find them, place some halved bagels in a 300°F oven and bake 15 minutes. Allow to cool before using.

4 Cretan- or Mani-style dry bread rusks

1 clove garlic, peeled and halved

3 tablespoons extra-virgin olive oil

1 large tomato, peeled and grated

¼ cup crumbled feta cheese

1 teaspoon dried oregano

1 Sprinkle some water over each rusk to soften it slightly. Then firmly rub the garlic clove over each rusk to infuse it with garlic flavor.

2 Drizzle oil evenly over rusks and let them absorb the oil for 5 minutes.

3 Top rusks with tomato, feta, and a sprinkle of oregano. Serve at room temperature.

Spinach Carbonara

Spinach adds iron, calcium, and vitamins to this otherwise rich dish. Turkey bacon is used here in place of the usual pork, but you could also use a soy substitute if you prefer a meatless version.

4 large egg yolks

½ cup grated pecorino Romano cheese

½ pound turkey bacon, chopped

⅓ cup water

1 tablespoon salt

8 ounces whole-wheat linguine

½ cup diced yellow onion

4 cloves garlic, peeled and smashed

¼ cup dry white wine

6 cups baby spinach

2 teaspoons cracked black pepper

1 In a small bowl, whisk together egg yolks and pecorino Romano. Set aside.

2 Place bacon and water in a large skillet over medium-high heat. Bring to a boil and cook until crisp, about 5 minutes. Remove bacon from skillet and drain on paper towels.

3 Reduce heat to medium-low and add onion and garlic to the skillet. Sauté 3 minutes. Add wine and continue stirring to deglaze the pan. Simmer about 4 minutes until most of the liquid is gone. Remove from heat, stir in bacon, and set aside.

4 Fill a large pot or Dutch oven with water. Place over high heat and bring to a boil. Add salt and pasta and cook about 9 minutes until al dente. Reserve 1 cup pasta water, then drain.

5 Transfer pasta to the skillet and set over very low heat. Add egg yolk mixture and spinach and quickly toss to coat pasta. Add reserved water 1 tablespoon at a time until sauce is smooth and pasta is evenly coated.

6 Remove from heat, top with pepper, and serve immediately.

SERVES 4

Per Serving:

Calories	490
Fat	20g
Sodium	982mg
Carbohydrates	50g
Fiber	3g
Sugar	2g
Protein	28g

CARBONARA MAGIC

A proper carbonara contains no cream, relying on the tempered pasta water, egg yolks, and cheese to give the sauce a creamy result.

Pasta with Turkey Sausage and Broccolini

SERVES 4

Per Serving:

Calories	560
Fat	29g
Sodium	682mg
Carbohydrates	54g
Fiber	1g
Sugar	5g
Protein	19g

Re-create a restaurant favorite at home with some healthy tweaks. This dish can also be made with broccoli instead of broccolini.

2 (3-ounce) links sweet Italian turkey sausage

3 tablespoons extra-virgin olive oil, divided

1 tablespoon salt

½ pound broccolini, each stalk cut into 4 pieces

8 ounces whole-wheat penne or gemelli

1 cup diced yellow onion

3 cloves garlic, peeled and minced

½ cup grated Parmesan cheese

½ teaspoon crushed red pepper flakes

1. Remove the casings from the sausage and roll the meat into small meatballs.
2. Heat 1 tablespoon oil in a large skillet over medium-high heat. Add meatballs to the skillet and brown on all sides, 10–12 minutes. Remove meatballs with a slotted spoon and drain on paper towels. Set aside.
3. Fill a large pot or Dutch oven with water. Place over high heat and bring to a boil. Add salt and broccolini. Boil 2 minutes. Using a slotted spoon, remove broccolini and plunge in a bowl of ice water. Drain and set aside.
4. Add pasta to the same pot of water and boil 6 minutes.
5. Meanwhile, add remaining 2 tablespoons oil to the skillet and heat over medium heat. Sauté onion and garlic 5–6 minutes until onion is translucent. Remove from heat.
6. Once pasta is cooked, use a slotted spoon to transfer it to the skillet. Reserve pasta water in the pot.
7. Add meatballs, broccolini, and 1 cup reserved pasta water to the skillet. Stir over medium-low heat until a sauce forms and pasta and broccolini are coated. Add Parmesan and red pepper flakes and toss to combine.
8. Serve hot.

Lemon-Garlic Green Beans with Almonds

For more flavor, toast the almonds before adding: Spread them on a parchment-lined baking sheet and roast in a preheated 350°F oven 8–10 minutes until just golden.

3 teaspoons salt, divided

1 pound fresh green beans, trimmed

2 cloves garlic, peeled and minced

1 tablespoon grated lemon zest

1½ teaspoons lemon juice

¼ cup extra-virgin olive oil

½ cup minced fresh parsley

¼ teaspoon ground black pepper

½ cup sliced almonds

1 Bring a large pot of water to a boil over high heat. Add 2 teaspoons salt and green beans. Return to a boil and cook 6 minutes. Drain and rinse with cold water.

2 Transfer green beans to a large bowl and add garlic, lemon zest, lemon juice, oil, parsley, pepper, and remaining 1 teaspoon salt. Toss to coat.

3 Top with almonds and serve.

SERVES 4

Per Serving:

Calories	260
Fat	22g
Sodium	850mg
Carbohydrates	12g
Fiber	6g
Sugar	5g
Protein	6g

Warm Bean Salad with Cherry Tomatoes

SERVES 4

Per Serving:

Calories	360
Fat	31g
Sodium	810mg
Carbohydrates	16g
Fiber	6g
Sugar	8g
Protein	6g

MUSTARD'S ROLE

Mustard acts as an emulsifier in salad dressings—it brings together the oil and vinegar (or other acidic liquid) so that they stay mixed longer. It also adds a bit of flavor, so use your favorite type when you make a dressing from scratch.

Expand your salad horizons beyond lettuce and other greens. This hearty, fiber-filled salad is great for a weeknight dinner.

1 pint cherry tomatoes, halved

3 cloves garlic, peeled and smashed

2 tablespoons plus ⅓ cup extra-virgin olive oil, divided

3¾ teaspoons salt, divided

½ teaspoon ground black pepper, divided

1 pound fresh green beans, trimmed

1 tablespoon whole-grain mustard

1 teaspoon honey

1 tablespoon red wine vinegar

¼ cup finely chopped roasted almonds

¼ cup chopped fresh mint

½ teaspoon dried oregano

1 tablespoon sesame seeds

1 Preheat oven to 350°F.

2 Place tomatoes and garlic on a large baking sheet and drizzle with 2 tablespoons oil. Sprinkle with ½ teaspoon salt and ¼ teaspoon pepper. Roast 25–30 minutes or just until wrinkled. Remove from oven.

3 Meanwhile, fill a large saucepan with water and bring to a boil over high heat. Add 3 teaspoons salt and green beans. Cook 5 minutes, then drain and rinse briefly with cold water. Set aside.

4 In a large bowl, whisk together mustard, honey, vinegar, and remaining ¼ teaspoon each salt and pepper. While continuing to whisk, pour in remaining ⅓ cup oil in a slow stream. Continue whisking until emulsified. Add green beans, tomatoes, almonds, mint, and oregano. Gently toss to coat.

5 Sprinkle salad with sesame seeds and serve immediately.

Spaghetti Puttanesca

SERVES 4

Per Serving:

Calories	340
Fat	11g
Sodium	752mg
Carbohydrates	56g
Fiber	3g
Sugar	8g
Protein	11g

TINY FLAVOR BOMBS

Caper bushes grow in arid regions of the Mediterranean. The immature green flower buds are picked, sun-dried, and then salted or brined. They add a tangy, briny flavor to all sorts of dishes.

You probably have everything you need to make this lively, spicy sauce right in your pantry. It's a great choice for a last-minute meal.

2 tablespoons extra-virgin olive oil

4 cloves garlic, peeled and minced

3 oil-packed anchovy fillets, drained and minced

2 cups plum tomato purée

¼ cup drained and rinsed nonpareil capers

16 pitted kalamata olives, sliced

½ cup chopped fresh parsley

2 teaspoons dried oregano

1 tablespoon salt

8 ounces whole-wheat spaghetti

½ teaspoon crushed red pepper flakes

1 Heat oil in a large skillet over medium heat. Sauté garlic and anchovies 1 minute. Stir in tomato purée and bring just to a boil. Reduce heat to medium-low and simmer uncovered 12–15 minutes until thickened. Add capers, olives, parsley, and oregano and stir to combine. Simmer 2 minutes, then remove from heat.

2 Bring a large pot of water to a boil over high heat. Add salt and pasta. Cook pasta until al dente, about 6 minutes. Drain, then add to skillet. Toss to coat.

3 Top with red pepper flakes and serve.

Pasta with Cherry Tomatoes, Basil, and Feta

In just 20 minutes, you can have this fresh and simple dish on your table. Use any ripe chopped tomato if you can't find cherry tomatoes.

2 tablespoons extra-virgin olive oil

1 pint cherry tomatoes, halved

3½ teaspoons salt, divided

¼ teaspoon ground black pepper

4 cloves garlic, peeled and minced

1 pound whole-wheat fettuccine

1 cup sliced fresh basil

1½ cups crumbled feta cheese

½ cup plain low-fat Greek yogurt

½ teaspoon crushed red pepper flakes

1 Heat oil in a large skillet over medium heat. Add tomatoes, ½ teaspoon salt, and black pepper. Cover the skillet and cook 5 minutes. Uncover and mash tomatoes slightly to release their juices. Add garlic and cook 10 minutes until sauce thickens.

2 Meanwhile, fill a large pot two-thirds with water and place over medium-high heat. Add remaining 3 teaspoons salt and bring to a boil. Add pasta and cook 6–7 minutes until al dente. Reserve ¼ cup pasta water, then drain.

3 Add pasta to sauce and stir to combine. If the sauce is a little thin or dry, stir in reserved pasta water. Stir in basil.

4 In a medium bowl, combine feta, yogurt, and red pepper flakes. Mash everything together with a fork. Add feta mixture to pasta and stir until sauce is creamy.

5 Serve immediately.

SERVES 8

Per Serving:

Calories	340
Fat	13g
Sodium	502mg
Carbohydrates	40g
Fiber	1g
Sugar	6g
Protein	15g

BASIL

The word *basil* in Greek is *basilikos*, which means "king." In the Mediterranean, there's no doubt that basil is the king of herbs. There are many varieties to be found, so try as many as you can to find your favorite.

Watermelon Caesar Salad

SERVES 4

Per Serving:

Calories	190
Fat	11g
Sodium	950mg
Carbohydrates	21g
Fiber	4g
Sugar	14g
Protein	6g

WHAT IS TAJÍN?

Tajín Clásico Seasoning is made with mild chili peppers, lime, and salt. It's often used as a seasoning on juicy fruits and vegetables. If you can't find it, look for another chili-lime seasoning powder or use a combination of chili powder, sea salt, and a squeeze of lime.

In the Mediterranean area, sweet, juicy watermelon is often paired with salty feta cheese. This flavor combination is the basis of a twist on a classic Caesar salad.

¼ cup crumbled feta cheese

1 tablespoon Worcestershire sauce

½ teaspoon ground black pepper

1 clove garlic, peeled and minced

1 teaspoon Dijon mustard

1 tablespoon lemon juice

¼ cup evaporated milk

2 tablespoons extra-virgin olive oil

1 large head romaine lettuce, cored and chopped

4 cups cubed seeded watermelon

⅓ cup sliced red onion

4 teaspoons chopped fresh mint

4 teaspoons Tajín Clásico Seasoning

1 Place feta, Worcestershire sauce, pepper, garlic, mustard, and lemon juice in a blender and process on high speed until smooth. Add milk and oil and process again until combined. Set aside.

2 Place lettuce in a large bowl and top with feta dressing. Toss to coat. Divide lettuce among four bowls or plates.

3 Top with watermelon, onion, and mint. Sprinkle with Tajín and serve immediately.

CHAPTER 5
Salads and Salad Dressings

Arugula Salad with Cabbage and Apple

SERVES 4

Per Serving:

Calories	150
Fat	11g
Sodium	390mg
Carbohydrates	11g
Fiber	2g
Sugar	6g
Protein	1g

This fiber-rich salad is delicious and satisfying, with bright, fresh flavors.

1 cup shredded green cabbage

1 large tart green apple, cored and shredded

1 tablespoon lemon juice

2 tablespoons extra-virgin olive oil

1 tablespoon white wine vinegar

½ teaspoon minced garlic

¼ teaspoon salt

¼ teaspoon ground black pepper

3 cups baby arugula

12 pitted kalamata olives

1 Place cabbage and apple in a medium bowl and sprinkle with lemon juice.

2 In the bottom of a large bowl, whisk together oil, vinegar, garlic, salt, and pepper. Add cabbage mixture and arugula and toss to coat.

3 Top salad with olives and serve.

Romaine Salad with Scallions and Dill

It takes minutes to make this simple but delicious salad. Make it your go-to side salad for any healthy meal.

6 cups chopped romaine lettuce

4 scallions, trimmed and thinly sliced

⅓ cup finely chopped fresh dill

3 tablespoons extra-virgin olive oil

1½ tablespoons red wine vinegar

½ teaspoon salt

¼ teaspoon ground black pepper

1 In a large salad bowl, combine lettuce, scallions, and dill.

2 In a small bowl, whisk together oil, vinegar, salt, and pepper. Pour over lettuce mixture and toss to coat.

3 Serve immediately.

SERVES 4

Per Serving:

Calories	120
Fat	11g
Sodium	300mg
Carbohydrates	4g
Fiber	1g
Sugar	2g
Protein	2g

AN ESSENTIAL KITCHEN TOOL

If you make salads regularly, it's a good idea to buy a good salad spinner. It gets your greens cleaner and drier than hand washing, and salad dressing clings better to drier lettuce.

Spinach Salad with Pomegranate Seeds

SERVES 4

Per Serving:

Calories	240
Fat	21g
Sodium	430mg
Carbohydrates	10g
Fiber	3g
Sugar	4g
Protein	4g

This salad is a twist on the classic spinach salad with pomegranate seeds providing a nice pop of flavor.

1 tablespoon Dijon mustard

1 teaspoon dried tarragon

3 tablespoons red wine vinegar

¼ cup extra-virgin olive oil

½ teaspoon salt

¼ teaspoon ground black pepper

4 cups baby spinach

1 cup thinly sliced red onion

½ cup sliced button mushrooms

⅓ cup roughly chopped toasted walnuts

⅓ cup pomegranate seeds

2 large hard-cooked eggs, peeled and quartered

1 In a large salad bowl, whisk together mustard, tarragon, and vinegar. Slowly pour in oil while whisking until emulsified. Stir in salt and pepper.

2 Add spinach, onion, mushrooms, walnuts, and pomegranate seeds. Toss gently. Top with eggs before serving.

Baby Greens with Chickpea Dressing

Puréed chickpeas are the base for this creamy, unusual salad dressing.

¼ cup drained and rinsed canned chickpeas

2 cloves garlic, minced

1 small shallot, peeled and minced

¼ cup chopped fresh parsley

½ teaspoon ground black pepper

½ cup balsamic vinegar

¼ cup extra-virgin olive oil

5 ounces baby salad greens

SERVES 6

Per Serving:

Calories	120
Fat	10g
Sodium	25mg
Carbohydrates	7g
Fiber	1g
Sugar	4g
Protein	1g

1 In a food processor, purée chickpeas. Add garlic, shallot, parsley, pepper, and vinegar; pulse until well incorporated.

2 With processor running, slowly add oil and process until mixture emulsifies.

3 Place greens in a large salad bowl. Top with chickpea dressing and toss. Serve immediately.

Spinach Salad with Apples and Mint

Use any variety of apples you like for this salad, but make sure you include at least one tart apple.

1 large orange

1 large grapefruit

⅓ cup extra-virgin olive oil

10 fresh mint leaves, chopped

1 tablespoon lime juice

¾ teaspoon salt

¼ teaspoon ground black pepper

1 large red apple, cored and sliced

1 large green apple, cored and sliced

⅓ cup finely chopped red onion

1 stalk celery, chopped

5 ounces baby spinach

1 Cut a small slice from the bottom and top of orange. Place orange on a cutting board, resting on one of the flat ends. Using a sharp knife, cut off the peel and pith, following the curve of the orange. Hold the peeled orange over a medium bowl and use the knife to cut between the membranes to release the sections. Set orange sections aside. Repeat with the grapefruit.

2 Process oil and mint in a food processor until well incorporated. Set aside and let the mint infuse the oil.

3 In a large bowl, whisk together reserved orange and grapefruit juices, lime juice, salt, pepper, and olive oil–mint infusion. Add apple slices, onion, and celery; toss to coat.

4 Add spinach and toss again to combine. Top salad with orange and grapefruit segments and serve.

SERVES 8

Per Serving:

Calories	150
Fat	10g
Sodium	240mg
Carbohydrates	16g
Fiber	3g
Sugar	11g
Protein	1g

A VERSATILE SALAD

Almost any kind of fruit would work well in this salad. Try peaches, plums, or cherries in the summer or a mixture of berries anytime.

Kale Salad with Peanut Dressing

SERVES 6

Per Serving:

Calories	120
Fat	10g
Sodium	170mg
Carbohydrates	5g
Fiber	2g
Sugar	2g
Protein	4g

ANCHOVY PASTE

Anchovy paste is usually found in the seafood section of most grocery stores. It's a good alternative to anchovy fillets if you're not likely to use up the leftovers in a can or jar of anchovies. To substitute, use $1/2$ teaspoon anchovy paste for each anchovy in a recipe. The paste lasts for a long time in the refrigerator.

If you've avoided kale salads because of kale's tough, chewy texture, try baby kale. You can find the baby version in clear clamshell packages in the produce section.

2 tablespoons smooth peanut butter

2 tablespoons warm water

2 tablespoons red wine vinegar

$1\frac{1}{2}$ teaspoons honey

1 clove garlic, peeled and minced

1 tablespoon lemon juice

1 tablespoon minced fresh ginger

1 teaspoon sesame oil

2 small oil-packed anchovy fillets, drained

$\frac{1}{4}$ teaspoon salt

$\frac{1}{4}$ teaspoon ground black pepper

5 ounces baby kale

$\frac{1}{3}$ cup finely chopped fresh mint

$\frac{1}{2}$ cup roughly chopped toasted walnuts

1 Place peanut butter, water, vinegar, honey, garlic, lemon juice, ginger, sesame oil, anchovies, salt, and pepper in a food processor or blender. Process until smooth.

2 In a large salad bowl, combine kale, mint, and walnuts. Top with peanut butter mixture and toss to coat.

3 Serve immediately.

Romaine Salad with Fennel, Orange, and Olives

Fennel has a mild licorice flavor. It's great in salads and adds a nice zing when paired with citrus fruit.

2 large oranges

2 tablespoons red wine vinegar

⅓ cup extra-virgin olive oil

½ teaspoon salt

¼ teaspoon ground black pepper

1 large head romaine lettuce

6 scallions, trimmed and thinly sliced

1 cup thinly sliced fennel

¼ cup chopped fennel fronds

1 cup thinly sliced radicchio

1 cup pitted kalamata olives

1 Cut a small slice from the bottom and top of 1 orange. Place orange on a cutting board, resting on one of the flat ends. Using a sharp knife, cut off the peel and pith, following the curve of the orange. Hold the peeled orange over a medium bowl and use the knife to cut between the membranes to release the sections. Set orange sections aside. Repeat with the second orange.

2 To the orange juice in the bowl, add vinegar, oil, salt, and pepper. Whisk to combine.

3 Place lettuce, scallions, fennel, fennel fronds, and radicchio in a large salad bowl. Top with dressing and toss to coat. Top with orange segments and olives. Serve immediately.

SERVES 6

Per Serving:

Calories	220
Fat	18g
Sodium	440mg
Carbohydrates	15g
Fiber	5g
Sugar	8g
Protein	2g

SUPREMES

The process of cutting away peel, pith, and membranes of a citrus fruit is called "supreming." You can use this technique whenever you add oranges or grapefruit to a salad.

Tomato Salad with Roasted Garlic Dressing

This easy-to-make salad is a nice addition to any summer meal.

SERVES 8

Per Serving:

Calories	150
Fat	14g
Sodium	420mg
Carbohydrates	6g
Fiber	1g
Sugar	3g
Protein	2g

ROASTED GARLIC AT HOME

To make your own roasted garlic: Remove the outer papery peel. Use a sharp knife to cut 1/2" off the top of the bulb. Place the bulbs, cut side up, in a small baking dish. Drizzle with a teaspoon of olive oil and cover with foil. Roast 30–40 minutes at 400°F until the cloves are softened. Roasted garlic will keep in the refrigerator 3–4 days in a covered container. You can also freeze roasted garlic: Place cloves on a baking sheet and freeze until solid. Then transfer to a zip-top plastic freezer bag.

4 large ripe tomatoes, cored and cut into wedges
½ medium red onion, peeled and thinly sliced
¾ teaspoon salt
½ teaspoon ground black pepper
2 tablespoons roasted garlic paste
⅓ cup pine nuts, toasted
½ cup sliced fresh basil
¼ cup extra-virgin olive oil
¼ cup sliced kalamata olives

1 In a large bowl, gently toss tomatoes, onion, salt, and pepper.
2 Place garlic paste, pine nuts, and basil in a mortar. Using a pestle, grind ingredients to make a paste. Add oil and mix to combine.
3 Add dressing to tomato mixture. Gently toss to coat. Top salad with olives and serve.

Politiki Cabbage Salad

This dish comes from the Byzantine city of Constantinople, or modern-day Istanbul. Because cabbage is so plentiful in the Mediterranean, cabbage salads are common fare.

1 teaspoon sugar

¾ teaspoon salt, divided

¼ cup red wine vinegar

4 cups shredded white cabbage

½ cup grated carrot

½ cup thinly sliced red bell pepper

¼ cup diced celery

¼ cup extra-virgin olive oil

⅛ teaspoon crushed red pepper flakes

½ teaspoon ground black pepper

1 In a large bowl, whisk together sugar, ½ teaspoon salt, and vinegar. Add cabbage, carrot, bell pepper, and celery and toss to combine. Set aside 15 minutes.

2 Using your hands, squeeze out excess liquid from the vegetables and transfer the vegetables to a separate large bowl.

3 Add oil, red pepper flakes, black pepper, and remaining ¼ teaspoon salt and toss to coat vegetables. Refrigerate until cold or serve at room temperature.

SERVES 6

Per Serving:

Calories	110
Fat	9g
Sodium	310mg
Carbohydrates	5g
Fiber	2g
Sugar	3g
Protein	1g

ALMOST PICKLES

When sugar, salt, and vinegar are combined, together they can quick-cure vegetables, as in this recipe.

Artichoke Salad

For a variation, try topping this salad with grilled calamari or shrimp.

PREVENT BROWNING

Be sure to have a bowl of acidulated water to place the peeled artichokes into. Acidulated water is water with acid added, usually lemon juice. The acidity in the water will keep the artichokes from browning.

- 2 medium yellow onions, peeled and chopped, divided
- 1 medium carrot, peeled and diced, divided
- 1 tablespoon finely chopped celery
- 2 tablespoons lemon juice
- 1½ teaspoons salt, divided
- 8 medium artichokes, outer layers peeled, trimmed, halved, and chokes removed
- 6 tablespoons extra-virgin olive oil, divided
- 1 medium red bell pepper, seeded and chopped
- 2 medium zucchini, trimmed and diced
- ½ cup fresh or frozen green peas
- ½ teaspoon ground black pepper
- 10 kalamata olives, sliced
- ¼ cup finely chopped drained capers
- ½ cup chopped fresh mint

1. Have a large bowl of ice water ready as an ice bath.
2. Add 3" water to a large, deep skillet and bring to a boil over medium-high heat. Add 2 tablespoons onion, 1 tablespoon carrot, celery, lemon juice, and 1 teaspoon salt. Return to a boil.
3. Add artichokes and reduce heat to medium-low. Cook artichokes 2 minutes until tender. Remove artichokes with a slotted spoon and place them in the ice bath to stop the cooking process. Discard the cooking liquid. When the artichokes have cooled, remove them from the ice bath and reserve.
4. Heat 2 tablespoons oil in a large skillet over medium-high heat. Add remaining onions, remaining carrot, and bell pepper. Reduce heat to medium and cook 5–6 minutes until vegetables are slightly softened. Add zucchini and cook 2 minutes. Add peas and cook another 2 minutes. Season with black pepper and remaining ½ teaspoon salt. Remove from heat and cool 15 minutes.
5. In a medium bowl, combine onion mixture, remaining 4 tablespoons oil, olives, capers, and mint.
6. To serve, place 3–4 artichoke halves on each plate and top with onion mixture. Serve at room temperature.

Raw Asparagus Salad

Top this salad with your favorite cheese or finely chopped nuts.

1 pound asparagus, rinsed and trimmed

½ teaspoon salt

1 tablespoon lemon juice

1 clove garlic, peeled and minced

1 tablespoon grated lemon zest

1 teaspoon fresh thyme leaves

2 tablespoons chopped fresh parsley

½ teaspoon ground black pepper

3 tablespoons extra-virgin olive oil

1 Using a vegetable peeler, shave asparagus into long, thin strips. In a medium bowl, combine shaved asparagus, salt, and lemon juice. Set aside 15 minutes.

2 In a small bowl, whisk together garlic, lemon zest, thyme, parsley, pepper, and oil.

3 Add dressing to asparagus and toss to coat. Refrigerate until cold or serve at room temperature.

SERVES 6

Per Serving:

Calories	80
Fat	7g
Sodium	200mg
Carbohydrates	4g
Fiber	2g
Sugar	2g
Protein	2g

SUPER ASPARAGUS

Add more asparagus to your diet. It's high in fiber and full of nutrients like folate and vitamins A, C, and K. It is also filling and low in calories.

Carrot Salad with Ouzo-Maple Dressing

SERVES 4

Per Serving:

Calories	350
Fat	23g
Sodium	890mg
Carbohydrates	30g
Fiber	3g
Sugar	23g
Protein	6g

This raw carrot salad is good any time of year, but especially in the wintertime, when it can be a challenge to find good vegetables.

3 large carrots, peeled

½ cup chopped fresh parsley

1 tablespoon Dijon mustard

2 tablespoons lemon juice

2 tablespoons red wine vinegar

2 tablespoons maple syrup

1 tablespoon ouzo

¼ cup extra-virgin olive oil

1 teaspoon salt

½ teaspoon ground black pepper

½ cup dried cranberries

⅓ cup shelled unsalted pistachios

½ cup crumbled feta cheese

1 Using the side of a box grater with large holes, use long strokes to shred carrots. Place shredded carrots in a medium bowl and add parsley.

2 In a small bowl, whisk together mustard, lemon juice, vinegar, maple syrup, and ouzo. Add oil, salt, and pepper and whisk again. Pour dressing over carrot mixture and toss to combine.

3 Cover and refrigerate 30 minutes. Remove from refrigerator and top with cranberries, pistachios, and feta before serving.

Tomato Salad with Purslane and Onion

Purslane is a leafy green with a slightly tangy taste that makes a wonderful, healthy addition to salads. It is high in fiber and one of the few greens that contain omega-3 fatty acids.

6 large ripe tomatoes, cored and cut into small wedges

¾ teaspoon salt, divided

1 cup purslane leaves and upper stems

½ cup thinly sliced red onion

3 tablespoons extra-virgin olive oil

4 teaspoons red wine vinegar

1 Place tomato wedges in a large bowl and sprinkle with ½ teaspoon salt. Set aside 10 minutes.

2 Add purslane, onion, oil, and vinegar and toss to combine. Sprinkle with remaining ¼ teaspoon salt and serve.

SERVES 4

Per Serving:

Calories	150
Fat	11g
Sodium	460mg
Carbohydrates	13g
Fiber	4g
Sugar	8g
Protein	3g

Cucumber Salad

SERVES 4

Per Serving:

Calories	250
Fat	25g
Sodium	750mg
Carbohydrates	4g
Fiber	1g
Sugar	2g
Protein	3g

This salad comes in handy during the summer months, when the garden is teeming with cucumbers. Cucumbers often play a supporting role in salads, but here they are the stars. Use a good-quality Greek feta cheese and crumble it yourself.

1 large cucumber

2 scallions, trimmed and chopped (green parts only)

¼ cup chopped fresh lemon verbena

½ cup crumbled feta cheese

6 tablespoons extra-virgin olive oil

3 tablespoons lemon juice

1 teaspoon coarse sea salt

½ teaspoon ground black pepper

1 Use a vegetable peeler to remove a strip of peel from cucumber from top to bottom. Turn cucumber slightly and peel another strip, leaving a strip of green peel in between peeled sections. Repeat until you've completed a green and white pattern around the circumference of the cucumber. Thinly slice cucumber and place in a medium bowl.

2 Add scallions, lemon verbena, feta, oil, lemon juice, and salt. Toss to coat. Sprinkle with pepper and serve immediately.

Brussels Sprout Leaf Salad

Raw Brussels sprout leaves are tender and very much edible. Studies show they can reduce the risk of cancer, decrease inflammation, and improve blood sugar control.

1 pound Brussels sprouts

¼ cup thinly sliced red onion

½ cup dried cherries or cranberries

⅓ cup sliced almonds

1 tablespoon lemon juice

2 tablespoons orange juice

1 tablespoon pink grapefruit juice

1 tablespoon red wine vinegar

¼ cup extra-virgin olive oil

1 teaspoon Dijon mustard

1 tablespoon honey

¼ teaspoon salt

¼ teaspoon ground black pepper

SERVES 6

Per Serving:

Calories	210
Fat	13g
Sodium	140mg
Carbohydrates	23g
Fiber	5g
Sugar	13g
Protein	5g

1 Cut through the stem side of each Brussels sprout. Discard tough outer leaves, then separate remaining leaves and place in a large bowl. Add onion, dried cherries, and almonds.

2 Place lemon juice, orange juice, grapefruit juice, vinegar, oil, mustard, honey, salt, and pepper in a glass jar with a lid and shake to emulsify.

3 Pour dressing over salad and toss to coat. Serve immediately.

Black-Eyed Pea Salad

SERVES 4

Per Serving:

Calories	350
Fat	29g
Sodium	530mg
Carbohydrates	20g
Fiber	5g
Sugar	7g
Protein	4g

Black-eyed peas are filling, loaded with fiber, and easy to cook. They make a great alternative to meat. Canned black-eyed peas will work if you're in a rush. Use 2 1/2 cups, drained and rinsed.

1 cup dried black-eyed peas

1½ teaspoons salt, divided

¾ cup diced red onion

½ cup diced red bell pepper

½ cup diced yellow bell pepper

½ cup diced celery

1 cup diced English cucumber

1 large ripe tomato, cored and diced

2 cups baby spinach leaves

1 cup finely chopped fresh parsley

¼ cup finely chopped fresh mint

1 tablespoon Dijon mustard

1 teaspoon honey

2 tablespoons red wine vinegar

2 tablespoons lemon juice

½ cup extra-virgin olive oil

¼ teaspoon ground black pepper

1 Place black-eyed peas in a large bowl and cover with 3 cups cold water. Set aside to soak overnight. The next day, drain peas and transfer to a medium saucepan. Add enough cold water to cover, then place over medium-high heat. Bring to a boil, then immediately drain peas and return to the pan. Add 5 cups fresh water and 1 teaspoon salt. Bring to a boil over high heat. Reduce heat to medium-low and simmer 30–45 minutes until tender. Drain and transfer peas to a large bowl.

2 Add onion, bell peppers, celery, cucumber, tomato, spinach, parsley, and mint and stir gently.

3 Place mustard, honey, vinegar, lemon juice, oil, black pepper, and remaining ½ teaspoon salt in a jar with a lid and shake until emulsified. Pour dressing over salad and toss to coat. Serve warm or at room temperature.

Avocado, Tomato, and Feta Salad

SERVES 4

Per Serving:

Calories	270
Fat	26g
Sodium	400mg
Carbohydrates	10g
Fiber	5g
Sugar	4g
Protein	5g

When it's too hot to cook, make this cool salad with ripe tomatoes, crunchy cucumbers, creamy avocado, and salty feta.

2 large tomatoes, cored and sliced

½ small red onion, peeled and thinly sliced

1 clove garlic, peeled and minced

2 tablespoons red wine vinegar

¼ cup extra-virgin olive oil

⅛ teaspoon table salt

1 large ripe avocado, peeled, pitted, and sliced

1 tablespoon lemon juice

4 large romaine lettuce leaves

½ cup crumbled feta cheese

¼ teaspoon coarse sea salt

¼ teaspoon ground black pepper

1 tablespoon chopped fresh oregano leaves

1 In a medium bowl, combine tomatoes, onion, garlic, vinegar, oil and table salt and toss to coat. Set aside 15 minutes.

2 Place avocado slices on a plate and sprinkle with lemon juice.

3 Arrange lettuce leaves on a platter in a single layer. Remove tomatoes and onion from the bowl with a slotted spoon and place on top of lettuce. Reserve the liquid in the bowl.

4 Top with avocado slices and feta, then drizzle with the reserved vinegar mixture. Sprinkle with sea salt, pepper, and oregano. Serve immediately.

Arugula, Sweet Potato, and Feta Salad

Arugula is a bitter green, but baby arugula is much milder and recommended for this colorful salad.

1½ pounds sweet potatoes, peeled

5 tablespoons extra-virgin olive oil, divided

¾ teaspoon salt, divided

½ teaspoon ground black pepper, divided

4 cups baby arugula

5 scallions, trimmed and thinly sliced

1½ tablespoons red wine vinegar

2 tablespoons chopped fresh mint

½ cup crumbled feta cheese

1   Place sweet potatoes in a large saucepan, cover with water, and bring to a boil over high heat. Reduce heat to medium and simmer 12 minutes. Drain sweet potatoes and set aside to cool 30 minutes.

2   Preheat broiler. Line a large baking sheet with parchment paper.

3   Dice sweet potatoes and place on prepared baking sheet. Drizzle with 2 tablespoons oil and season with ½ teaspoon salt and ¼ teaspoon pepper. Toss to coat. Broil 5 minutes until just browned around the edges. Transfer to a large bowl. Add arugula and scallions.

4   In a small bowl, whisk together remaining 3 tablespoons oil, vinegar, mint, and remaining ¼ teaspoon each salt and pepper. Gently toss to coat, then top with feta.

5   Serve immediately.

SERVES 4

Per Serving:

Calories	380
Fat	22g
Sodium	690mg
Carbohydrates	39g
Fiber	7g
Sugar	13g
Protein	7g

SALTY AND SWEET

Salty and sweet flavor combinations are everywhere! Think kettle corn, peanut butter and jelly, chocolate-covered pretzels, or bacon-topped doughnuts. Here's a new one for the list: sweet potatoes and feta cheese. Once you try it, you'll be hooked!

Grilled Onion and Arugula Salad with Walnuts

SERVES 4

Per Serving:

Calories	320
Fat	28g
Sodium	630mg
Carbohydrates	15g
Fiber	3g
Sugar	7g
Protein	7g

OVEN-ROASTED ONIONS

Roasted onions will work just as well as grilled onions. Place onion slices on a baking sheet lined with parchment paper. Drizzle with oil and season as directed. Roast at 450°F 15 minutes.

Onions contain natural sugars that reduce and caramelize when cooked, combining the flavors of savory and sweet. Throw some whole onions on the grill next time you have a barbecue, and your salad is halfway done.

4 medium yellow onions, peeled and cut into 3 crosswise slices

4 tablespoons extra-virgin olive oil, divided

¼ teaspoon ground black pepper

¾ teaspoon salt, divided

4 cups baby arugula

1 teaspoon fresh thyme leaves

1 tablespoon red wine vinegar

1 clove garlic, peeled and minced

½ cup crumbled feta cheese

½ cup roughly chopped toasted walnuts

1 Preheat a charcoal or gas grill.

2 Brush both sides of onion slices with 2 tablespoons oil and season with pepper and ½ teaspoon salt. Grill 7–8 minutes per side until softened and slightly charred. Remove from grill and chop roughly. Set aside.

3 In a large salad bowl, combine arugula and thyme.

4 In a small bowl, whisk together remaining 2 tablespoons oil, vinegar, garlic, and remaining ¼ teaspoon salt. Pour over arugula mixture and toss to coat.

5 Top salad with onions, feta, and walnuts. Serve immediately.

Roasted Beet and Almond Salad

Earthy beets are roasted, poached in a vinegar mixture, and paired with a luscious herbed goat cheese in this entrée-sized salad. Keep the poaching liquid to use for a future salad dressing.

4 medium beets

½ cup plus 1 tablespoon red wine vinegar, divided

½ cup balsamic vinegar

2 ounces goat cheese, softened

1 teaspoon chopped fresh mint

1 teaspoon chopped fresh thyme

2 tablespoons chopped fresh chives

½ teaspoon ground black pepper, divided

1 tablespoon lemon juice

2 tablespoons orange juice

1 tablespoon pink grapefruit juice

¼ cup extra-virgin olive oil

1 teaspoon Dijon mustard

1 tablespoon honey

¼ teaspoon salt

4 cups mixed salad greens

¼ cup toasted sliced almonds

SERVES 4

Per Serving:

Calories	280
Fat	20g
Sodium	290mg
Carbohydrates	16g
Fiber	2g
Sugar	13g
Protein	5g

PEELING TIP

To peel roasted beets, use the dull side of a butter knife. The skins will slip off.

1 Preheat oven to 400°F.

2 Place beets in a roasting pan just large enough to contain them. Pour in 1" water. Roast 60–75 minutes until tender when pierced with a fork. Remove beets from the pan and cool on a rack at least 30 minutes. Peel beets and cut into ¼" slices.

3 Place ½ cup red wine vinegar and balsamic vinegar in a medium saucepan and bring to a boil over medium-high heat. Add beets and poach 2 minutes. Remove beets with a slotted spoon and set aside to cool.

4 In a medium bowl, place cheese, mint, thyme, chives, and ¼ teaspoon pepper. Using a wooden spoon, mix until combined. Transfer mixture to a large piece of plastic wrap. Form into a log and wrap tightly in plastic wrap. Refrigerate at least 1 hour.

5 Place lemon juice, orange juice, grapefruit juice, remaining 1 tablespoon red wine vinegar, oil, mustard, honey, salt, and remaining ¼ teaspoon pepper in a glass jar and shake to emulsify.

6 In a large bowl, toss greens with dressing until coated. Divide greens among four salad plates and top with sliced beets.

7 Remove herbed goat cheese from the refrigerator and cut into four slices. Add a slice to each salad. Top with almonds and serve.

Chopped Asparagus Salad

Nothing says spring like a light and fresh asparagus salad. If you prefer your asparagus slightly cooked, blanch the spears in boiling water 2 minutes, then immediately immerse them in ice water.

1 bunch asparagus, trimmed and cut into 1" pieces

2 large Roasted Red Peppers (see recipe in Chapter 11), diced

½ cup thinly sliced red onion

1 pint cherry tomatoes, halved

1 teaspoon Dijon mustard

1 tablespoon red wine vinegar

3 tablespoons balsamic vinegar

⅓ cup extra-virgin olive oil

¼ teaspoon salt

⅛ teaspoon ground black pepper

½ cup roughly chopped walnuts

¼ cup crumbled feta cheese

1 In a large bowl, combine asparagus, Roasted Red Peppers, onion, and tomatoes.

2 In a small bowl, whisk together mustard, red wine vinegar, balsamic vinegar, oil, salt, and black pepper. Pour over vegetables and toss to coat.

3 Top with walnuts and feta and serve immediately.

SERVES 4

Per Serving:

Calories	340
Fat	30g
Sodium	580mg
Carbohydrates	13g
Fiber	4g
Sugar	8g
Protein	6g

LOVE OF OLIVE OIL

The most characteristic aspect of the Mediterranean diet is the ubiquitous presence of the olive and its oil in the foods that comprise the traditional cuisines that evolved under its influence.

Warm Mushroom Salad

SERVES 8

Per Serving:

Calories	230
Fat	22g
Sodium	350mg
Carbohydrates	5g
Fiber	2g
Sugar	2g
Protein	4g

This is a wonderful hearty winter salad. King mushrooms, used in many Mediterranean dishes, are thick and meaty. If you can't find them, use portobello mushrooms instead.

⅔ cup extra-virgin olive oil, divided

2 cups sliced cremini mushrooms

2 cups sliced king mushrooms

6 cloves garlic, peeled and smashed

2 bay leaves

1 teaspoon chopped fresh rosemary

1 teaspoon fresh thyme leaves

1 teaspoon salt, divided

½ teaspoon ground black pepper, divided

1 teaspoon Dijon mustard

2 tablespoons balsamic vinegar

1 tablespoon lemon juice

5 ounces spring mix salad greens

¼ cup shelled pumpkin seeds

½ cup crumbled goat cheese

1 Heat ⅓ cup oil in a large cast iron pan or heavy skillet over medium-low heat 30 seconds. Add mushrooms, garlic, bay leaves, rosemary, thyme, ½ teaspoon salt, and ¼ teaspoon pepper. Cook 20 minutes, stirring occasionally. Remove and discard bay leaves.

2 In a small jar with a lid, place remaining ⅓ cup oil, mustard, vinegar, lemon juice, and remaining ½ teaspoon salt and ¼ teaspoon pepper. Close the jar and shake vigorously until dressing is emulsified.

3 In a large bowl, add greens and dressing and toss to combine. Divide greens among eight plates and top with mushrooms. Sprinkle salad with pumpkin seeds and cheese. Serve warm or at room temperature.

Warm Lentil Salad

Serve this salad with poached fish fillets or roasted shrimp. For a fresh taste, squeeze a bit of lemon juice over the salad.

3 tablespoons extra-virgin olive oil

¼ cup minced shallots

½ cup finely chopped carrot

½ cup finely chopped celery

2 cups dried lentils

2 sprigs fresh oregano

2 sprigs fresh parsley

1 bay leaf

4 cups vegetable stock

1 teaspoon salt

½ teaspoon ground black pepper

1 Heat oil in a large saucepan or Dutch oven over medium-high heat. Sauté shallots, carrots, and celery until soft and translucent, 2–3 minutes.

2 Add lentils, oregano, parsley, bay leaf, and stock. Bring to a boil. Cover, reduce heat to medium-low, and simmer 30–40 minutes until almost all the liquid has evaporated.

3 Remove and discard herb sprigs and bay leaf. Season with salt and pepper and serve.

SERVES 4

Per Serving:

Calories	460
Fat	12g
Sodium	870mg
Carbohydrates	69g
Fiber	11g
Sugar	7g
Protein	24g

Butternut Squash Salad

This unusual salad is an "autumn surprise," with ribbons of raw butternut squash as the main ingredient. The dressing's acidity brightens the flavor of the squash, and the slightly salty Parmesan shavings are irresistible.

1 medium (about 2½-pound) butternut squash

¾ teaspoon salt

¼ teaspoon ground black pepper

2 tablespoons lemon juice

½ teaspoon Dijon mustard

¼ cup extra-virgin olive oil

1 cup shaved Parmesan cheese

½ cup pomegranate seeds

1 cup toasted pecan halves

1 Cut squash with a knife, separating the narrow neck from the wider end. Reserve the wider end for another use. Use a vegetable peeler to remove the peel, then run the peeler along the length of the squash to make thin strips of squash.

2 In a large bowl, sprinkle squash ribbons with salt and pepper and toss to coat. Set aside 5 minutes.

3 In a small bowl, whisk together lemon juice, mustard, and oil. Pour over squash and toss to coat.

4 Top salad with Parmesan, pomegranate seeds, and pecan halves. Serve immediately.

Green Olive Dressing

Green olives aren't just for martinis. They make a great dressing for mixed greens or steamed vegetables.

2 oil-packed anchovy fillets, drained

1 teaspoon grated lemon zest

1½ teaspoons lemon juice

½ cup roughly chopped red onion

2 cloves garlic, peeled and smashed

3 tablespoons red wine vinegar

1 cup roughly chopped fresh parsley

1 cup pitted green olives

2 teaspoons drained and rinsed capers

½ cup extra-virgin olive oil

1 Place anchovies, lemon zest, lemon juice, onion, and garlic in a food processor or blender and process until smooth.

2 Add vinegar, parsley, olives, and capers. Pulse until chunky. Continue to pulse while adding a steady stream of olive oil. Serve at room temperature or refrigerate up to 1 week.

MAKES 2 CUPS

Per Serving (2 tablespoons):

Calories	80
Fat	8g
Sodium	200mg
Carbohydrates	1g
Fiber	0g
Sugar	0g
Protein	0g

TAME THE SALT

If your olives are too salty, place them in a bowl and cover them with cold water. Drain them after 30 minutes, and the salt in the olives will be reduced.

Pomegranate Vinaigrette

SERVES 8

Per Serving:

Calories	270
Fat	28g
Sodium	230mg
Carbohydrates	4g
Fiber	0g
Sugar	4g
Protein	0g

Toss this dressing with baby dandelion greens and top with crumbled feta or goat cheese. Pomegranate molasses can be found in Greek and Middle Eastern grocers.

½ cup unsweetened pomegranate juice

1 clove garlic, peeled and minced

1 cup extra-virgin olive oil

¾ teaspoon salt

⅓ teaspoon ground black pepper

1 teaspoon Dijon mustard

2 tablespoons pomegranate molasses

1 Combine all ingredients in a jar with a lid. Close the jar and shake it vigorously until ingredients are emulsified.

2 Serve at room temperature or refrigerate up to 1 week.

Tofu Tzatziki

Experiment with the type of tofu you use for this creamy tzatziki. Medium tofu will give you a thinner mixture, and firm tofu will make the sauce thicker. If you can find medium-firm tofu, the sauce will be creamy, but not too thick. Find your own version of "just right."

1 cup grated English cucumber

¾ teaspoon salt, divided

8 ounces medium or firm tofu, drained

2 cloves garlic, peeled and minced

1 tablespoon red wine vinegar

2 tablespoons extra-virgin olive oil

2 tablespoons chopped fresh dill

1 Place cucumber in a colander and sprinkle with ½ teaspoon salt. Set aside to drain 1 hour. Use your hands to squeeze out excess water from cucumber and transfer to a medium bowl.

2 In a food processor or blender, add tofu, garlic, vinegar, oil, and remaining ¼ teaspoon salt. Process until smooth. Pour over cucumber and stir to combine. Add dill and stir again.

3 Cover and refrigerate at least 1 hour before serving. Serve cold.

MAKES 1½ CUPS

Per Serving (2 tablespoons):

Calories	40
Fat	3g
Sodium	135mg
Carbohydrates	1g
Fiber	0g
Sugar	0g
Protein	2g

MIX IT UP

Tzatziki typically contains fresh dill. But other fresh herbs can create a whole new flavor profile. Try mint, oregano, or lemon verbena.

Vegan Yogurt Tzatziki

MAKES 3 CUPS

**Per Serving
(2 tablespoons):**

Calories	20
Fat	1g
Sodium	0mg
Carbohydrates	2g
Fiber	0g
Sugar	1g
Protein	1g

Serve with wedges of pita bread or in a vegetarian gyro.

1½ cups plain vegan soy yogurt
1 tablespoon extra-virgin olive oil
1 tablespoon lemon juice
4 cloves garlic, peeled and minced
2 medium cucumbers, peeled and grated
1 tablespoon chopped fresh mint

1 In a small bowl, whisk together yogurt, oil, and lemon juice until combined. Stir in garlic, cucumbers, and mint.
2 Cover and refrigerate at least 1 hour before serving. Serve cold.

CHAPTER 6
Plant-Based Main Dishes

Arakas Laderos (Greek-Style Peas)

SERVES 4

Per Serving:

Calories	240
Fat	14g
Sodium	310mg
Carbohydrates	22g
Fiber	9g
Sugar	9g
Protein	8g

This vegetarian dish of green peas, tomatoes, and mint is one of a group of Greek dishes called ladera, *which means "in oil."*

3 tablespoons extra-virgin olive oil, divided

1 tablespoon unsalted butter

4 scallions, trimmed and thinly sliced

18 ounces fresh or frozen green peas

2 medium tomatoes, grated

3 tablespoons chopped fresh dill

½ teaspoon salt

½ teaspoon ground black pepper

1 cup hot water

1 tablespoon chopped fresh mint

1 Heat 2 tablespoons oil in a medium skillet over medium heat. Add butter and scallions. Cook 2 minutes until scallions are softened.

2 Add peas and cook another 2 minutes.

3 Add tomatoes, dill, salt, pepper, and hot water. Cover and cook 30 minutes or until all liquid is absorbed and only the oil remains.

4 Serve warm topped with mint and remaining 1 tablespoon oil.

Cauliflower Stifado

This is a vegetarian version of stifado, a dish usually made with beef. Stifado *in Greek refers to a dish with lots of onions. In this version, pearl onions provide sweetness.*

1/4 cup extra-virgin olive oil

1 medium head cauliflower, cored and cut into florets

1 medium yellow onion, peeled and sliced

4 cloves garlic, peeled and minced

2 bay leaves

1 large red bell pepper, seeded and chopped

1 1/2 tablespoons tomato paste

3 tablespoons chopped fresh rosemary

1 cup peeled pearl onions

6 small red potatoes, halved

3 cups vegetable stock

3/4 teaspoon salt

1/2 teaspoon ground black pepper

4 cups chopped kale

1 cup pitted kalamata olives

1 teaspoon dried oregano

1 tablespoon red wine vinegar

1 Heat oil in a large pot or Dutch oven over medium-high heat. Add cauliflower florets and cook 5 minutes or until browned. Remove cauliflower with a slotted spoon and set aside.

2 Reduce heat to medium and add yellow onion, garlic, bay leaves, and bell pepper to the pot. Cook 5–6 minutes. Add tomato paste, rosemary, pearl onions, and potatoes. Stir and cook 1 minute.

3 Add stock, salt, and black pepper. Cover pot and simmer 20 minutes.

4 Uncover pot and add cauliflower and kale. Cover pot and simmer 10 minutes until kale wilts. Add olives. Simmer uncovered 5 minutes until sauce has thickened.

5 Stir in oregano and vinegar. Remove and discard bay leaves. Serve hot.

SERVES 6

Per Serving:

Calories	320
Fat	15g
Sodium	720mg
Carbohydrates	44g
Fiber	7g
Sugar	9g
Protein	7g

PEELING PEARL ONIONS

To easily remove skins from pearl onions, make a cross into the root side with a sharp knife, boil them 1 minute, then plunge them in ice water. The skins will slide right off.

Chestnut Stifado

SERVES 6

Per Serving:

Calories	370
Fat	15g
Sodium	390mg
Carbohydrates	52g
Fiber	4g
Sugar	7g
Protein	6g

You can now find cooked, vacuum-packed chestnuts online and at many grocery stores. They are tender, sweet, and a great addition to this stew. Serve it with some crusty whole-grain bread.

6 tablespoons extra-virgin olive oil, divided

12 pearl onions, peeled

1 medium yellow onion, peeled and sliced

10 ounces ready-to-eat roasted chestnuts

1 pound cremini or button mushrooms, halved

2 cloves garlic, peeled and smashed

3 large sweet potatoes, peeled and cut into large chunks

3 tablespoons tomato paste

1/2 cup tomato purée

1/2 cup dry white wine

3 bay leaves

6 whole allspice berries

3/4 teaspoon salt

1/2 teaspoon ground black pepper

1 tablespoon red wine vinegar

1 Heat 4 tablespoons oil in a deep, wide skillet over medium-high heat. Sauté pearl onions 5–7 minutes until lightly browned. Add sliced onion, chestnuts, mushrooms, and garlic. Reduce heat to medium. Sauté 5 minutes.

2 Stir in sweet potatoes, tomato paste, tomato purée, wine, bay leaves, allspice berries, salt, and pepper. Add remaining 2 tablespoons oil and enough hot water to almost cover all the ingredients. Bring to a boil. Reduce heat to low, cover, and simmer 30–40 minutes until pearl onions and sweet potatoes are fork-tender.

3 Remove from heat and remove and discard bay leaves. Stir in vinegar and serve.

Fassolakia Ladera (Braised Green Beans with Potatoes and Tomatoes)

Fassolakia Ladera can be made with any kind of green beans. The flavorful tomato sauce infuses the long-cooked green beans and potatoes. Add a green salad, and you have dinner!

½ cup extra-virgin olive oil

3 medium yellow onions, peeled and sliced

5 cloves garlic, peeled and sliced

¾ teaspoon salt, divided

3 cups tomato purée

4 whole allspice berries

2 pounds green beans, trimmed

½ cup chopped fresh parsley

¼ cup chopped fresh mint

½ cup chopped fresh dill

6 large russet potatoes, peeled and halved

1 cup hot water

½ teaspoon ground black pepper

1 Place oil, onions, garlic, and ¼ teaspoon salt in a large saucepan. Stir to combine, cover, and cook 5–7 minutes until onions are softened. Add tomato purée and allspice berries and simmer another 5 minutes.

2 Add green beans, parsley, mint, dill, potatoes, and hot water. Increase heat to high and bring to a boil. Reduce heat to medium-low and simmer 45 minutes or until green beans and potatoes are tender. Season with remaining ½ teaspoon salt and pepper.

3 Serve immediately.

SERVES 8

Per Serving:

Calories	440
Fat	15g
Sodium	430mg
Carbohydrates	72g
Fiber	9g
Sugar	12g
Protein	10g

TOMATO PURÉE

Canned tomato purée is fine for this dish, but if you have some fresh ripe tomatoes, make your own purée. Grate 3–4 large tomatoes using the larger holes on a box grater. Discard the skins before using.

Baked Gigante Beans

SERVES 6

Per Serving:

Calories	180
Fat	5g
Sodium	460mg
Carbohydrates	26g
Fiber	2g
Sugar	4g
Protein	8g

BRUSCHETTA

Turn leftovers into an appealing appetizer. Toast small slices of Italian or French bread, then rub them with a cut garlic clove. Reheat the leftover beans and spoon a bit onto each piece of bread.

Although this dish is easy to make, it's an impressive and delicious one with oversized, creamy gigante beans. These giants may be labeled elephant beans or butter beans at the store.

1 pound dried gigante beans, rinsed and picked through

1 large carrot, peeled, halved lengthwise, and cut into ½" pieces

1 large stalk celery, diced

3 bay leaves

3 cloves garlic, peeled and smashed

2 tablespoons extra-virgin olive oil

2 large yellow onions, peeled and chopped

½ cup tomato purée

1½ tablespoons tomato paste

½ teaspoon smoked paprika

1 teaspoon salt

½ teaspoon ground black pepper

1 cup chopped fresh parsley

¼ cup chopped fresh dill

1 Place beans in a large saucepan or Dutch oven and add enough water to cover. Bring to a boil over high heat. Reduce heat to medium and cook 2 minutes. Drain beans and return to the pot.

2 Add carrot, celery, bay leaves, and garlic. Add enough water to cover ingredients by 1". Bring to a boil over high heat. Reduce heat to medium and cook for 45 minutes or until beans are softened. Using a slotted spoon, transfer the bean mixture to a large casserole dish. Reserve the liquid from the beans.

3 Preheat oven to 375°F.

4 Heat oil in a large skillet over medium heat. Add onions and sauté about 5 minutes or until softened. Stir in tomato purée, tomato paste, paprika, salt, pepper, and parsley. Add to the bean mixture in the casserole dish and stir to combine.

5 Pour in enough of the reserved liquid to cover everything in the casserole dish. Bake 30 minutes.

6 Remove the dish from oven and stir in dill. Return dish to oven and bake another 10–15 minutes until most of the liquid is gone and the top is just golden. Remove and discard bay leaves.

7 Serve hot or at room temperature.

Chickpeas with Leeks and Spinach

Slightly sweet and richly flavored, balsamic vinegar isn't just for salads. It adds a unique flavor to this vegetarian stew.

2 tablespoons extra-virgin olive oil

2 cups sliced leeks

3 cloves garlic, peeled and minced

4 cups drained and rinsed canned chickpeas

2 bay leaves

2 cups tomato sauce

1 cup finely chopped fresh parsley

2 tablespoons balsamic vinegar

½ teaspoon salt

½ teaspoon ground black pepper

4 cups baby spinach

¼ cup chopped fresh mint

SERVES 4

Per Serving:

Calories	360
Fat	11g
Sodium	1,240mg
Carbohydrates	53g
Fiber	14g
Sugar	11g
Protein	15g

1 Heat oil in a large saucepan over medium-high heat. Sauté leeks and garlic 5 minutes. Stir in chickpeas, bay leaves, tomato sauce, parsley, vinegar, salt, and pepper. Add enough hot water to just cover the contents. Bring to a boil.

2 Reduce heat to low, cover, and simmer 30 minutes. Remove from heat.

3 Remove and discard bay leaves.

4 Stir in spinach and mint. Serve immediately.

Artichokes with Peas and Carrots

SERVES 6

Per Serving:

Calories	300
Fat	5g
Sodium	650mg
Carbohydrates	57g
Fiber	18g
Sugar	9g
Protein	13g

Fresh green peas can be hard to find. Use frozen peas instead. All they need is a quick rinse; you don't need to defrost them.

2 tablespoons extra-virgin olive oil

2 cups diced yellow onions

2 medium carrots, peeled, halved lengthwise, and sliced

12 medium fresh or frozen artichokes, outer layers peeled, trimmed, halved, and chokes removed

4 medium Yukon Gold potatoes, peeled and quartered

2 tablespoons lemon juice

1 teaspoon salt

½ teaspoon ground black pepper

1½ cups fresh or frozen green peas

1 cup finely chopped fresh dill, divided

2 tablespoons chopped fresh mint

1 Heat oil in a large saucepan over medium-high heat. Sauté onions and carrots 5 minutes.

2 Add artichokes, potatoes, lemon juice, salt, pepper, and enough water to cover. Bring to a boil. Reduce heat to medium-low, cover, and simmer 30–35 minutes until artichokes and potatoes are fork-tender.

3 Add peas and ½ cup dill. Cover and simmer another 10 minutes. Remove from heat.

4 Stir in mint and remaining ½ cup dill.

5 Serve warm.

Sympetherio (Beans and Lentils with Bulgur)

A dish like this makes it easy to forgo meat. Fava beans, chickpeas, navy beans, and bulgur wheat make this dish fortifying, filling, and delicious.

½ cup medium-coarse bulgur

1½ cups water

1 teaspoon salt, divided

2 tablespoons extra-virgin olive oil

1 small yellow onion, peeled and diced

1 cup drained and rinsed canned fava beans

1 cup drained and rinsed canned chickpeas

1 cup drained and rinsed canned navy beans

1 cup drained and rinsed canned lentils

¼ teaspoon ground black pepper

1 tablespoon lemon juice

½ cup finely chopped fresh parsley

¼ cup finely chopped fresh dill

SERVES 6

Per Serving:

Calories	220
Fat	8g
Sodium	470mg
Carbohydrates	38g
Fiber	3g
Sugar	2g
Protein	11g

1 Place bulgur in a small saucepan with water and ½ teaspoon salt. Bring to a boil over high heat, then reduce heat to medium-low, cover, and simmer 14 minutes. Fluff with a fork and set aside to cool 15 minutes.

2 Heat oil in a medium skillet over medium-high heat. Sauté onion 5–6 minutes until translucent. Remove from heat and transfer to a large bowl.

3 Add fava beans, chickpeas, navy beans, lentils, cooked bulgur, remaining ½ teaspoon salt, pepper, lemon juice, parsley, and dill. Stir to combine.

4 Serve at room temperature or refrigerate at least 2 hours and serve cold.

Gemista (Baked Stuffed Vegetables)

Stuffed vegetables are made regularly in the summer months in Greece. Of course you can make this in the cooler months, but this dish shines with ripe, locally grown vegetables.

SERVES 6

Per Serving:

Calories	410
Fat	15g
Sodium	990mg
Carbohydrates	53g
Fiber	5g
Sugar	9g
Protein	7g

6 medium tomatoes

6 medium bell peppers

¼ cup plus 2 tablespoons extra-virgin olive oil, divided

12 scallions, trimmed and thinly sliced

4 cloves garlic, peeled and minced

2 cups long-grain white rice

1 cup chopped fresh dill

1 cup chopped fresh parsley

¼ cup chopped fresh mint

½ teaspoon ground black pepper

2½ teaspoons salt, divided

1 Preheat oven to 400°F.
2 With a small, sharp knife, slice the top off each tomato and bell pepper, reserving the tops. Use the knife to cut the inner membranes of the peppers and remove seeds, leaving the outer shells intact. Carefully spoon out the flesh of each tomato into a medium bowl, leaving the outer shell intact, and set aside.
3 Place tomatoes and peppers in a 13" × 9" baking dish. The vegetables should fit tightly so that they don't topple over. Use a smaller baking dish if necessary.
4 Place tomato pulp in a food processor or blender and pulse to purée. Transfer to a medium bowl. Add ¼ cup oil, scallions, garlic, rice, dill, parsley, mint, black pepper, and 2 teaspoons salt and stir to combine.
5 Using a spoon, stuff each vegetable with the rice mixture, pushing the filling down with your fingers if necessary. Cover with the reserved tops.
6 Drizzle with remaining 2 tablespoons oil and sprinkle with remaining ½ teaspoon salt. Bake uncovered 60–70 minutes until vegetables are golden brown on top.
7 Serve warm or at room temperature.

Briam (Greek Roasted Vegetables)

Briam could be one of the original "one-pot" meals. All you need to do is cut up some vegetables and layer the ingredients in a roasting pan. It's a great summer dish for when no one wants to be in the kitchen all day.

SERVES 6

Per Serving:

Calories	240
Fat	10g
Sodium	460mg
Carbohydrates	35g
Fiber	7g
Sugar	11g
Protein	6g

4 tablespoons extra-virgin olive oil, divided

3 medium russet potatoes, peeled and sliced

1 large eggplant, trimmed and sliced

3 medium zucchini, trimmed and sliced

6 cloves garlic, peeled and sliced

1 large carrot, peeled and sliced

2 medium yellow onions, peeled and thinly sliced, divided

1 cup chopped fresh parsley, divided

1 teaspoon salt, divided

¾ teaspoon ground black pepper, divided

2 medium tomatoes, cored and sliced

1 large red bell pepper, seeded and sliced

1 medium Cubanelle pepper, seeded and sliced

½ cup tomato purée

4 scallions, trimmed and chopped

3 bay leaves

2 teaspoons dried oregano

3 cups water

1 Preheat oven to 425°F. Brush a large roasting pan with 2 tablespoons oil.

2 Layer potato slices on the bottom of prepared pan, followed by a layer of eggplant slices and a layer of zucchini slices. Top with garlic, carrot, and half the onion slices. Sprinkle with ½ cup parsley and ½ teaspoon each salt and black pepper.

3 Add a layer of tomato slices, bell pepper, and Cubanelle pepper, then remaining onion slices. Top with tomato purée, scallions, bay leaves, and oregano. Carefully pour water over the vegetables.

4 Drizzle with remaining 2 tablespoons oil and season with remaining ½ teaspoon salt and ¼ teaspoon black pepper.

5 Bake 1 hour until the top is golden brown and the liquid has thickened. Remove and discard bay leaves. Sprinkle with remaining parsley before serving.

Imam Bayildi (Turkish Stuffed Eggplant)

Per Serving:

Calories	300
Fat	11g
Sodium	710mg
Carbohydrates	50g
Fiber	19g
Sugar	25g
Protein	8g

WHY DID THE IMAM FAINT?

The literal translation of *imam bayildi* is "the imam fainted." It's unclear why he fainted. Some say it's because the dish was so delicious that he was overcome. Others think he fainted at the cost of the dish. Either way, it is a swoon-worthy dish.

This casserole is delicious served at room temperature on a hot day.

1 sprig fresh thyme

6 whole allspice berries

6 small eggplants, trimmed and cut in half lengthwise

4 tablespoons olive oil, divided

1½ teaspoons salt, divided

4 medium yellow onions, peeled and sliced

1 large green bell pepper, seeded and sliced

1 (14.5-ounce) can whole tomatoes, hand crushed

2 teaspoons dried oregano

10 cloves garlic, peeled and thinly sliced

½ cup chopped fresh parsley

½ teaspoon ground black pepper

3 medium fresh tomatoes, cored and thinly sliced

1 medium red onion, peeled and thinly sliced

1 Create a bouquet garni: Place a square of cheesecloth on a table. Place thyme sprig and allspice berries in the center. Gather up the edges of the cloth and tie together with twine. Set aside.

2 Preheat oven to 400°F. Line a large baking sheet with parchment paper.

3 Place eggplant halves on a work surface, cut sides up. Use a sharp knife to score the flesh of the eggplants, forming a crosshatch pattern. Be careful not to cut through the peel. Drizzle eggplant halves with 2 tablespoons oil and sprinkle with 1 teaspoon salt. Place cut side down on prepared baking sheet and bake 30 minutes. Remove from oven; leave oven on.

4 Meanwhile, heat the remaining 2 tablespoons oil in a large skillet over medium-high heat. Add yellow onions and bell pepper and sauté 5–7 minutes until softened. Add crushed tomatoes, oregano, and bouquet garni. Bring to a boil. Reduce heat to low, cover, and simmer 20–25 minutes until the liquid has been absorbed. Remove the bouquet garni. Add garlic, parsley, black pepper, and remaining ½ teaspoon salt.

5 Transfer eggplant to one or two baking dishes large enough to hold them side by side, placing cut side up. Use a spoon or ladle to press down into each half to form a depression. Spoon the tomato mixture over the eggplant halves. Top with sliced fresh tomato and red onion.

6 Bake 45–60 minutes until golden brown. Cool 15 minutes. Serve.

Orecchiette with Rapini and Bread Crumbs

Rapini is a bitter green full of iron and fiber. The toasted bread crumbs temper the bitterness. Small pasta shells work well in this dish if you cannot find orecchiette.

1 pound rapini, trimmed

1 tablespoon salt

8 ounces whole-wheat orecchiette

4 tablespoons extra-virgin olive oil, divided

2 (1-ounce) slices Italian bread, torn into crumbs

½ cup diced yellow onion

4 cloves garlic, peeled and minced

½ teaspoon crushed red pepper flakes

SERVES 4

Per Serving:

Calories	430
Fat	18g
Sodium	452mg
Carbohydrates	60g
Fiber	7g
Sugar	3g
Protein	15g

1. Cut rapini in half and separate the ends with the leaves from the stem ends. Cut the stem ends into 1" pieces.
2. Fill a large pot with water and add salt. Bring to a boil over high heat. Add rapini stems and boil 2 minutes. Add the leaf ends and boil another 2 minutes. Use a strainer or slotted spoon to remove rapini from the water (do not discard water). Set aside.
3. Add pasta to the same pot of water and bring back to a boil. Cook 8 minutes, then drain and set aside.
4. Meanwhile, heat 2 tablespoons oil in a large skillet over medium heat. Add bread crumbs and stir constantly until golden brown, about 3 minutes. Remove bread crumbs from skillet and set aside.
5. Wipe the skillet clean, add remaining 2 tablespoons oil, and heat over medium heat. Add onion and garlic and sauté 7 minutes until translucent.
6. Drain pasta, reserving 1 cup cooking water. Add pasta and rapini to the skillet and toss to incorporate. If necessary, add some of the reserved pasta water to increase the volume of sauce.
7. Top with bread crumbs and red pepper flakes before serving.

Vegetarian Gyros

WELL-TRAVELED FRUITS

Did you know peppers are fruits, not vegetables? Peppers originated in Mexico and South America and were introduced to Spain in the late 1400s. They were quickly adopted by and grown in other European countries. From there, peppers spread to Africa and Asia.

Smoky, garlicky grilled vegetables take the place of sliced meat in these easy-to-make summer wraps. Topped with chickpeas, juicy tomatoes, and a creamy sauce, these gyros are destined to become favorites at your house.

2 large portobello mushrooms, cut into thick slices

1 medium red onion, peeled and cut into thick slices

2 large zucchini, trimmed and cut lengthwise into slices

2 large red bell peppers, seeded and cut into quarters

¼ cup extra-virgin olive oil

2 tablespoons lemon juice

2 cloves garlic, peeled and minced

2 teaspoons dried oregano

1 teaspoon salt

¼ teaspoon ground black pepper

6 (6½") pita rounds, warmed

6 tablespoons Vegan Yogurt Tzatziki (see recipe in Chapter 5)

1 medium tomato, cored and diced

1 cup drained and rinsed canned chickpeas

¼ cup finely chopped fresh parsley

1 teaspoon paprika

1 Preheat a gas or charcoal grill.

2 Place mushrooms, onion, zucchini, and bell peppers in a large bowl. In a small bowl, combine oil, lemon juice, garlic, oregano, salt, and black pepper. Whisk to combine, then pour over vegetables. Toss to coat.

3 Grill vegetables 5 minutes on each side, brushing with remaining marinade.

4 To assemble each gyro, place a sheet of foil on a flat surface and top with 1 warm pita. Make sure the top 1" of the pita extends over the top edge of the foil. Spoon grilled vegetables onto the middle of the pita and top with Vegan Yogurt Tzatziki, tomato, chickpeas, parsley, and paprika.

5 Roll the foil and pita together to form a cone shape, leaving the top end open. Serve immediately.

Grilled Eggplant and Zucchini with Feta and Mint

SERVES 4

Per Serving:

Calories	320
Fat	28g
Sodium	570mg
Carbohydrates	14g
Fiber	5g
Sugar	9g
Protein	4g

There's no need to get rid of your grill if you're reducing your meat intake. Grilled vegetables are smoky, vibrant, and delicious.

1 large eggplant, trimmed and sliced lengthwise into ¼" slices

2 medium zucchini, trimmed and sliced lengthwise into ¼" slices

2 tablespoons plus ⅓ cup extra-virgin olive oil, divided

¼ teaspoon ground black pepper

¾ teaspoon salt, divided

3 tablespoons balsamic vinegar

1 clove garlic, peeled and minced

1 teaspoon Dijon mustard

¼ cup chopped fresh mint

1 tablespoon chopped fresh parsley

¼ cup crumbled feta cheese

1 Preheat a gas or charcoal grill.
2 Brush eggplant and zucchini slices with 2 tablespoons oil. Sprinkle with pepper and ½ teaspoon salt. Grill 3 minutes per side, then transfer to a large platter.
3 In a small jar with a lid, combine remaining ⅓ cup oil, vinegar, garlic, mustard, and remaining ¼ teaspoon salt. Close the jar and shake vigorously until emulsified.
4 Spoon dressing over grilled vegetables and sprinkle with mint and parsley. Top with feta.
5 Serve warm or at room temperature.

Potatoes Yiachni

In Greece and Turkey, yiachni *refers to a one-pot dish cooked on the stovetop. Vegetarian versions of yiachni are often made during Greek Orthodox fasting periods, when many Christians avoid meat in their diets.*

⅓ cup extra-virgin olive oil

1 medium yellow onion, peeled and roughly chopped

1 small red bell pepper, seeded and sliced

1 small green bell pepper, seeded and sliced

1 medium carrot, peeled, halved lengthwise, and sliced

2 cloves garlic, peeled and smashed

6 large Yukon Gold potatoes, peeled and quartered

¾ cup tomato purée

2 cups vegetable stock

1 teaspoon paprika

2 bay leaves

½ teaspoon crushed red pepper flakes

1 teaspoon dried oregano

1½ teaspoons salt

½ teaspoon ground black pepper

SERVES 6

Per Serving:

Calories	420
Fat	13g
Sodium	700mg
Carbohydrates	72g
Fiber	2g
Sugar	6g
Protein	8g

1 Heat oil in a large pot or Dutch oven over medium-high heat. Sauté onion, bell peppers, and carrot 5–7 minutes until softened. Add garlic and sauté 30 seconds. Add potatoes, tomato purée, stock, paprika, bay leaves, red pepper flakes, oregano, salt, and black pepper.

2 Bring to a boil, then reduce heat to low and cover. Simmer 40 minutes, then uncover and cook another 5–10 minutes until sauce is thickened.

3 Remove from heat, remove and discard bay leaves, and cool 10 minutes before serving.

Mushroom Giouvetsi

SERVES 6

Per Serving:

Calories	330
Fat	7g
Sodium	630mg
Carbohydrates	55g
Fiber	7g
Sugar	11g
Protein	15g

Mushrooms do a great job of replacing meat in recipes. For more flavor, top Mushroom Giouvetsi with grated pecorino Romano cheese.

½ cup dried mushrooms

6 cups hot vegetable stock

2 tablespoons extra-virgin olive oil

1 large yellow onion, peeled and diced

1 medium carrot, peeled and grated

1 stalk celery, finely diced

2 cups sliced fresh mushrooms

2 cloves garlic, peeled and minced

¼ cup dry white wine

2 cups fresh or canned crushed tomatoes

2 bay leaves

1 teaspoon fresh thyme leaves

1 teaspoon dried oregano

½ teaspoon salt

½ teaspoon ground black pepper

8 ounces orzo

½ teaspoon ground nutmeg

¼ cup chopped fresh parsley

1. Place dried mushrooms in a large bowl and cover with stock. Set aside to soak 10 minutes. Drain mushrooms, reserving stock. Roughly chop mushrooms and set aside.

2. Heat oil in a large skillet over medium-high heat. Sauté onion, carrot, celery, and fresh mushrooms 5–7 minutes until softened. Add garlic and sauté 1 minute. Add wine, tomatoes, bay leaves, thyme, oregano, salt, and pepper. Bring to a boil. Reduce heat to medium-low and simmer 25–30 minutes until most of the liquid has been cooked down. Remove and discard bay leaves.

3. Increase heat to high and add orzo to the skillet. Cook, stirring, 5 minutes. Add chopped mushrooms and reserved stock. Bring to a boil, then remove from heat.

4. Preheat oven to 375°F.

5. Pour mushroom mixture into a large baking dish and sprinkle with nutmeg and parsley. Bake 45 minutes until most of the liquid has been absorbed and the top is golden brown.

6. Cool 10 minutes before serving.

Mushroom Fricassee

This dish is popular in southern France on the Mediterranean Sea. The food of this region resembles that of Italy or Greece more than Paris.

2 tablespoons extra-virgin olive oil

8 ounces white mushrooms, halved

1 cup diced yellow onion

3 cloves garlic, peeled and minced

½ cup diced carrot

10 ounces baby spinach

1½ cups vegetable stock

1 tablespoon lemon juice

1 teaspoon salt

½ teaspoon ground black pepper

1 teaspoon cornstarch

4 teaspoons cold water

½ cup finely chopped fresh parsley

½ cup finely chopped fresh dill

SERVES 4

Per Serving:

Calories	130
Fat	7g
Sodium	750mg
Carbohydrates	13g
Fiber	3g
Sugar	5g
Protein	4g

1 Heat oil in a large saucepan over medium-high heat. Sauté mushrooms 5–6 minutes until browned. Add onion, garlic, and carrot and reduce heat to medium. Sauté 5–6 minutes until softened.

2 Add spinach and stir until wilted.

3 Stir in stock, lemon juice, salt, and pepper. Cover and cook 20 minutes. Uncover and cook another 5 minutes.

4 In a small bowl, mix together cornstarch and cold water. Stir the mixture into the pot and cook 1–2 minutes until sauce thickens.

5 Top with parsley and dill and serve.

Ratatouille

SERVES 6

Per Serving:

Calories	60
Fat	2.5g
Sodium	150mg
Carbohydrates	11g
Fiber	1g
Sugar	5g
Protein	2g

SUMMER AND WINTER SQUASH

You will often hear yellow squash referred to as "summer squash." Squash is normally divided into two groups: summer squash and winter squash. Summer squashes have thin skins and soft seeds. Winter squashes have tough skins and hard seeds.

There are no limits to the types of vegetables that can be added to ratatouille. Get creative and experiment!

½ teaspoon extra-virgin olive oil
1 small eggplant, trimmed and chopped
1 small zucchini, trimmed and chopped
1 small yellow squash, trimmed and chopped
½ medium leek, trimmed and chopped
1 medium shallot, peeled and minced
2 cloves garlic, peeled and minced
1 medium plum tomato, cored and diced
1 tablespoon chopped fresh thyme
1 cup vegetable stock
¼ cup chopped kalamata olives
1 teaspoon ground black pepper

1 Heat oil in a large saucepan or Dutch oven over medium-high heat. Sauté eggplant, zucchini, yellow squash, leek, shallot, and garlic until slightly softened, about 8 minutes.
2 Add tomato, thyme, and stock. Bring to a boil, then reduce heat to low. Cover and simmer 20 minutes.
3 Add olives and pepper; cook another 5 minutes. Serve hot or at room temperature.

Chickpea Fritters in Pita

Chickpeas fritters are filling and nutritious, and they are great at room temperature or reheated as leftovers. If you like, wrap the fritters in sturdy lettuce leaves instead of pita bread.

1 (15-ounce) can chickpeas, drained and rinsed

1 cup sliced scallions

1 clove garlic, peeled

1 cup finely chopped fresh parsley

¼ cup chopped fresh dill

1 large egg

1 teaspoon salt

¼ teaspoon ground black pepper

½ cup all-purpose flour

¾ cup vegetable oil

4 (6½") pita rounds, warmed

½ cup sliced red onion

1 medium tomato, cored and sliced

½ cup diced cucumber

½ cup Vegan Yogurt Tzatziki (see recipe in Chapter 5)

2 tablespoons chopped fresh mint

SERVES 4

Per Serving:

Calories	520
Fat	22g
Sodium	1,160mg
Carbohydrates	66g
Fiber	9g
Sugar	9g
Protein	17g

1 Place chickpeas, scallions, garlic, parsley, dill, egg, salt, and pepper in a food processor and pulse until the mixture forms a smooth paste. Form the mixture into twelve small balls and place on a plate or baking sheet. Cover loosely and refrigerate at least 1 hour.

2 Place flour in a shallow bowl. Dredge fritters in flour and return to the plate or baking sheet.

3 Heat oil in a large skillet over medium-high heat. Fry fritters 8–10 minutes, turning often, until golden brown on all sides. Transfer to a paper towel–lined plate.

4 For each pita, place 1 pita round on a flat surface and top with three fritters. Top with onion, tomato, cucumber, and Vegan Yogurt Tzatziki. Fold pita in half and serve.

Vegetarian Moussaka

Although still a rich dish, this moussaka is a healthier and flavorful version of the original. Brown lentils replace the usual minced meat, and a whipped potato topping replaces the béchamel sauce.

SERVES 8

Per Serving:

Calories	480
Fat	14g
Sodium	1,230mg
Carbohydrates	65g
Fiber	10g
Sugar	9g
Protein	26g

1 large eggplant, trimmed and cut into ½" slices

2 large zucchini, trimmed and cut into ½" slices

4 tablespoons extra-virgin olive oil, divided

1½ teaspoons salt, divided

1 cup diced yellow onion

3 cloves garlic, peeled and minced

2 cups dried brown lentils, rinsed and picked through

3 cups tomato sauce

3 cups water

2 bay leaves

3 whole allspice berries

½ teaspoon ground black pepper

½ teaspoon dried oregano

4 medium Yukon Gold potatoes, peeled and cut into chunks

1 cup whole milk

½ cup plain whole-milk yogurt

2 large eggs

¼ teaspoon ground nutmeg

¾ cup grated pecorino Romano cheese, divided

1 cup dried plain bread crumbs

1 Preheat oven to 375°F.

2 Brush both sides of eggplant and zucchini slices with 2 tablespoons oil and sprinkle with ½ teaspoon salt. Place on a large baking sheet and bake 15 minutes. Flip slices and bake 10 minutes more. Transfer slices to metal rack and set aside to cool.

3 Heat the remaining 2 tablespoons oil in a large skillet over medium-high heat. Sauté onion and garlic 5 minutes. Add lentils, tomato sauce, water, bay leaves, allspice berries, pepper, and ½ teaspoon salt and bring to a boil. Reduce heat to medium-low and simmer 15–20 minutes until lentils are tender and sauce is thick. Remove and discard bay leaves and allspice berries. Stir in oregano. Set aside and keep warm.

4 Place potatoes and remaining ½ teaspoon salt in a medium sauce-pan. Add water to cover and bring to a boil over medium-high heat. Reduce heat to low, cover, and simmer 15 minutes until potatoes are fork-tender. Drain, then transfer to a large bowl. Mash potatoes roughly with a fork and set aside to cool 10 minutes. Add milk, yogurt, and eggs. With a handheld electric mixer, beat on medium speed until smooth. Stir in nutmeg and ½ cup pecorino Romano.

5 Sprinkle ⅓ cup bread crumbs on the bottom of a large, deep bak-ing dish. Layer eggplant slices over the bread crumbs. Cover with half the lentil mixture, then another ⅓ cup bread crumbs. Next, add zucchini slices, then remaining lentil mixture and remaining ⅓ cup bread crumbs.

6 Spoon the mashed potato mixture over the top of the casserole and smooth it with an offset spatula. Sprinkle with remaining ¼ cup pecorino Romano.

7 Bake 30–40 minutes until top is golden brown. Remove from oven and cool at least 30 minutes before serving.

Trahana with Mushroom Ragu

SERVES 4

Per Serving:

Calories	260
Fat	10g
Sodium	200mg
Carbohydrates	34g
Fiber	1g
Sugar	4g
Protein	7g

Trahana, one of the world's oldest foods, is a tiny, pebble-shaped grain product made of cracked wheat, eggs, and milk or yogurt. There are two types: sweet and sour. Sweet trahana is made with whole milk; sour trahana is made with buttermilk or yogurt. It can be found at Greek, Middle Eastern or Turkish specialty stores.

2 tablespoons extra-virgin olive oil

1 pound mixed mushrooms, sliced

¼ cup minced shallots

1 teaspoon tomato paste

¼ cup dry white wine

1 bay leaf

¼ teaspoon ground allspice

1½ cups vegetable stock, divided

2 teaspoons fresh thyme leaves

¼ teaspoon ground black pepper

¾ teaspoon salt, divided

1½ cups water

1 cup sour trahana

¼ cup shaved Parmesan cheese

1 Heat oil in a large skillet over medium heat. Sauté mushrooms 2 minutes. Add shallots and sauté 3 minutes. Stir in tomato paste and cook 1 minute more.

2 Add wine, bay leaf, allspice, and 1 cup stock and increase heat to high. Bring to a boil, then reduce heat to medium-low and simmer uncovered 15 minutes or until thickened. Remove and discard bay leaf. Stir in thyme, pepper, and ½ teaspoon salt. Set aside and keep warm.

3 Place water, remaining ½ cup stock, and remaining ¼ teaspoon salt in a medium saucepan. Bring to a boil over high heat. Stir in trahana and reduce heat to low. Cover and simmer, stirring occasionally, 8–10 minutes until most of the liquid has been absorbed.

4 Divide trahana among four shallow bowls. Top with mushrooms and sprinkle with Parmesan. Serve immediately.

Mushroom Ragu with Egg Noodles

There are so many mushrooms available today—from wild to farmed, fresh and dried, affordable and expensive. Use a combination of mushrooms that suits you.

2 tablespoons extra-virgin olive oil

5 cups sliced mushrooms, any variety

1 cup diced yellow onion

3 cloves garlic, peeled and minced

3 bay leaves

5 sprigs fresh thyme

¼ cup dry white wine

8 ounces wide egg noodles

2¼ cups low-fat milk

2⅔ cups vegetable stock

1 teaspoon salt

½ teaspoon ground black pepper

½ cup chopped fresh parsley

½ cup grated Parmesan cheese

SERVES 8

Per Serving:

Calories	220
Fat	7g
Sodium	520mg
Carbohydrates	30g
Fiber	1g
Sugar	7g
Protein	9g

1 Heat oil in a large saucepan or Dutch oven over medium-high heat. Sauté mushrooms 5 minutes. Add onion, garlic, bay leaves, and thyme and sauté another 7 minutes until onion is translucent.

2 Add wine and cook 2–3 minutes until absorbed. Add egg noodles, milk, stock, salt, and pepper. Bring to a boil.

3 Reduce heat to medium-low, cover, and simmer 20 minutes, stirring occasionally. Uncover and simmer another 5 minutes. Remove from heat. Remove and discard bay leaves and thyme sprigs.

4 Add parsley and Parmesan; toss to coat. Serve immediately.

Ladenia (Greek-Style Flatbread)

This thick-crust flatbread topped with vegetables is pure comfort food. Just don't call it pizza!

SERVES 8

Per Serving:

Calories	410
Fat	21g
Sodium	150mg
Carbohydrates	49g
Fiber	4g
Sugar	3g
Protein	7g

3 tablespoons light olive oil, divided

1 tablespoon semolina

1½ teaspoons active dry yeast

½ teaspoon sugar

1½ cups warm water (110°F)

½ teaspoon table salt

3½ cups all-purpose flour

4 tablespoons extra-virgin olive oil

2 large yellow onions, peeled and sliced

2 large tomatoes, cored, halved vertically, and cut into half-moon slices

½ teaspoon coarse sea salt

⅛ teaspoon ground black pepper

2 tablespoons dried oregano

1 Brush a 14" pizza pan with 1 tablespoon light olive oil and sprinkle with semolina. Set aside.

2 In a large bowl, combine yeast, sugar, and warm water. Set aside at room temperature 7–10 minutes until mixture starts to bubble. Stir in table salt and remaining 2 tablespoons light olive oil. Add about 2 cups flour and stir until incorporated. Continue adding flour while kneading on a floured work surface about 3–5 minutes until the dough is pliable and no longer sticky.

3 Roll out dough to a 14" circle and transfer to prepared pizza pan. Place in a warm spot to rise 30 minutes.

4 Preheat oven to 400°F.

5 Spread extra-virgin olive oil over the top of the dough. Top with onions and tomatoes. Sprinkle with coarse salt, pepper, and oregano.

6 Bake on the middle rack of the oven 40–45 minutes until lightly browned.

7 Serve hot or cold.

CHAPTER 7

Soups, Stews, and Chilis

Gazpacho

SERVES 6

Per Serving:

Calories	70
Fat	0g
Sodium	280mg
Carbohydrates	16g
Fiber	3g
Sugar	9g
Protein	2g

ICE CUBE GARNISH

Fill an ice cube tray's compartments with 1 tablespoon extra-virgin olive oil. Place the tray in the freezer to harden. Use them as a garnish for any cold savory soup. A bit of chopped herbs in the cubes will make them pretty and aromatic.

This soup makes a great showcase from your summer garden! Use only the freshest ingredients and remove the seeds from the vegetables.

2 large sweet onions, peeled and chopped

3 medium cucumbers, peeled and chopped

1½ pounds plum tomatoes, cored and chopped

3 cloves garlic, peeled and minced

½ cup chopped fresh cilantro

1 chipotle pepper in adobo sauce, drained and chopped

2 tablespoons lime juice

1½ teaspoons grated lime zest

¼ teaspoon hot pepper sauce

½ teaspoon ground black pepper

6 cups vegetable stock

1 In a large bowl, mix together onions, cucumbers, tomatoes, garlic, cilantro, chipotle pepper, lime juice, lime zest, pepper sauce, and black pepper. Transfer three-quarters of the mixture to a blender or food processor. Set aside remaining vegetables.

2 Purée mixture until smooth. Add stock and pulse until combined.

3 To serve, ladle into serving bowls and garnish with reserved vegetable mixture.

Cold Cucumber Soup

Make this soup when you have an abundance of cucumbers from your garden. It comes together quickly using a food processor.

3 medium cucumbers

2 cloves garlic, peeled and minced

1 tablespoon red wine vinegar

2 slices white bread, crusts removed, roughly torn

1½ cups plain low-fat yogurt

1½ cups cold water

3 tablespoons extra-virgin olive oil, divided

¼ cup plus 2 tablespoons chopped fresh dill, divided

¾ teaspoon salt

1 Peel and grate 2 cucumbers and set aside. Peel remaining cucumber and cut into ½" cubes. Set aside.

2 In a food processor, add garlic, vinegar, and bread. Process until mixture becomes a paste. Add grated cucumbers and yogurt and process again.

3 With the processor running, slowly add water in a steady stream. Add 2 tablespoons oil, ¼ cup dill, and salt. Pulse a few times to blend into the soup.

4 Transfer soup into a container with a lid. Cover it and refrigerate at least 2 hours until cold.

5 Before serving, stir the soup. Top with cubed cucumber and remaining 2 tablespoons dill. Drizzle soup with remaining 1 tablespoon oil.

SERVES 6

Per Serving:

Calories	110
Fat	8g
Sodium	350mg
Carbohydrates	8g
Fiber	1g
Sugar	2g
Protein	2g

Artichoke Soup

SERVES 8

Per Serving:

Calories	210
Fat	4g
Sodium	650mg
Carbohydrates	39g
Fiber	4g
Sugar	7g
Protein	6g

THICKENING WITHOUT CREAM

Adding potatoes to a soup allows the starches to help thicken the broth. You won't miss the cream!

Frozen artichokes let you skip the arduous prep work involved in preparing the vegetable. And you can have this full-flavored soup on your table in less than 45 minutes.

2 tablespoons extra-virgin olive oil

4 cups chopped leeks

10 cups vegetable stock

18 thawed frozen artichokes

3 large russet potatoes, peeled and quartered

2 tablespoons lemon juice

1 teaspoon salt

½ teaspoon ground black pepper

½ cup plain low-fat Greek yogurt

½ cup chopped fresh chives

1. Heat oil in a large stockpot over medium heat. Add leeks and cook, stirring occasionally, 10 minutes until softened.
2. Increase heat to high. Add stock, artichokes, and potatoes and bring to a boil. Reduce heat to medium-low. Simmer 40 minutes.
3. Remove from heat and use an immersion blender to purée the soup or transfer in batches to a blender to purée. Stir in lemon juice, salt, and pepper.
4. To serve, ladle into bowls and top each bowl with a spoonful of yogurt and a sprinkle of chives.

Chickpea Soup

Of course soaking dried chickpeas overnight in water will be superior, but canned chickpeas are wonderful, and your soup will be on the table in less than an hour.

2 tablespoons extra-virgin olive oil

2 cups diced yellow onions

1 medium carrot, peeled and finely diced

1 stalk celery, trimmed and finely diced

4 cloves garlic, peeled and minced

8 cups vegetable stock

4 cups drained and rinsed canned chickpeas

½ medium lemon, sliced

¼ cup chopped fresh parsley

3 bay leaves

1 teaspoon paprika

½ teaspoon dried oregano

¾ teaspoon salt

½ teaspoon ground black pepper

1 Heat oil in a large saucepan or Dutch oven over medium-high heat. Sauté onions, carrot, and celery 5–7 minutes until softened. Stir in garlic and sauté 1 minute. Add stock, chickpeas, lemon slices, parsley, bay leaves, and paprika and bring just to a boil. Reduce heat to medium-low and simmer, partially covered, 45 minutes.

2 Remove and discard bay leaves and season with oregano, salt, and pepper.

3 Serve immediately.

SERVES 6

Per Serving:

Calories	240
Fat	7g
Sodium	870mg
Carbohydrates	36g
Fiber	8g
Sugar	11g
Protein	8g

BAY LEAVES

Bay leaves provide a wonderful aroma and subtle flavor when added to dishes like soups and stews. Don't forget to remove bay leaves before serving.

Spring Vegetable Soup

SERVES 6

Per Serving:

Calories	130
Fat	1g
Sodium	270mg
Carbohydrates	26g
Fiber	10g
Sugar	12g
Protein	9g

SOUP FOR DINNER

Whether in Greece, Turkey, Italy, Morocco, Spain, Israel, or neighboring countries, a soup or broth can often be the main meal of the day.

This delicious vegetable-packed soup is perfect for springtime, when fresh asparagus is readily available and affordable at local grocers.

3 pounds asparagus

1 pound cauliflower

8 ounces carrots, peeled and sliced

8 ounces turnips, peeled and diced

8 ounces string beans, trimmed and sliced diagonally

1 cup fresh or frozen green peas

2 cups vegetable stock

¼ teaspoon salt

¼ teaspoon ground black pepper

½ cup chopped fresh cilantro

1 Spray a 4- to 5-quart slow cooker with nonstick cooking spray. Cut 2" tips from asparagus and florets from cauliflower and place in slow cooker; set aside asparagus stalks and cauliflower stems for use in other recipes.

2 Stir in carrots, turnips, beans, peas, stock, salt, and pepper. Cover and cook on low 3½ hours.

3 Stir in cilantro and cook 30 minutes more. Serve immediately.

Purée of Red Lentil Soup

SERVES 8

Per Serving:

Calories	230
Fat	4.5g
Sodium	410mg
Carbohydrates	35g
Fiber	9g
Sugar	4g
Protein	14g

Red lentils are a great source of fiber, they're inexpensive, and they can be stored in your pantry. Unlike many other legumes, they don't need presoaking and they cook rather quickly.

2 cups dried red lentils, rinsed and picked through

2 medium yellow onions, peeled and roughly chopped

1 large carrot, peeled, halved lengthwise, and roughly chopped

1 medium red bell pepper, seeded and chopped

¾ cup tomato sauce

1 tablespoon smoked paprika

3 bay leaves

6 cloves garlic, peeled and smashed

8 cups water

2 teaspoons dried oregano

1 teaspoon salt

½ teaspoon ground black pepper

2 tablespoons extra-virgin olive oil

1 Place lentils, onions, carrot, bell pepper, tomato sauce, paprika, bay leaves, garlic, and water in a large pot or Dutch oven. Cover and bring to a boil over high heat. Reduce heat to medium-low and simmer 45 minutes.

2 Remove from heat. Remove and discard bay leaves. Stir in oregano, salt, and black pepper. Purée soup with an immersion blender or transfer in batches to a blender and process until smooth.

3 Ladle soup into bowls and drizzle with oil before serving.

Cabbage Soup

Cabbage is hearty and filling. Make a pot of this soup and you'll find it remarkably satisfying.

2 tablespoons extra-virgin olive oil

2 cups diced yellow onions

1 large carrot, peeled and sliced

1 stalk celery, trimmed and diced

1 medium red bell pepper, seeded and diced

3 cloves garlic, peeled and minced

3 cups finely chopped cabbage

1 (15-ounce) can white navy beans, drained and rinsed

1 teaspoon smoked paprika

1 teaspoon fresh thyme leaves

¾ teaspoon salt

1 teaspoon ground black pepper

2 bay leaves

1½ cups tomato-vegetable juice (such as V8)

7 cups vegetable stock

1 small dried Calabrian chili pepper, roughly chopped

2 medium zucchini, trimmed, halved lengthwise, and sliced

SERVES 8

Per Serving:

Calories	140
Fat	7g
Sodium	740mg
Carbohydrates	29g
Fiber	3g
Sugar	9g
Protein	7g

1 In a large saucepan or Dutch oven, heat oil over medium-high heat. Sauté onions, carrot, celery, and bell pepper 7–10 minutes until softened. Stir in garlic and sauté 1 minute.

2 Add cabbage, beans, paprika, thyme, salt, black pepper, and bay leaves. Cook and stir 2 minutes.

3 Add juice, stock, and chili pepper and bring to a boil. Reduce heat to medium-low, cover, and simmer 45 minutes.

4 Add zucchini and simmer 5 minutes. Remove and discard bay leaves before serving.

Hearty Winter Vegetable Soup

SERVES 8

Per Serving:

Calories	150
Fat	4g
Sodium	660mg
Carbohydrates	27g
Fiber	3g
Sugar	8g
Protein	4g

LEEKS

Leeks are part of the onion family and are wonderful for making soups. They do need thorough cleaning, as dirt often gets in between the layers. To clean them properly, cut the ends off the leeks and cut them in half lengthwise. Run them under cold water while running your fingers back and forth between the layers to remove grit.

Serve this soup with crusty bread and a glass of red wine. It's wonderful when eaten by a warm fire.

2 tablespoons extra-virgin olive oil

1 large leek, trimmed, cut lengthwise, and sliced

5 cloves garlic, peeled and minced

2 large carrots, peeled and diced

3 stalks celery, trimmed and diced

1 large red bell pepper, seeded and diced

3 bay leaves

3 sprigs fresh thyme

1 teaspoon salt, divided

1 teaspoon ground black pepper, divided

1 medium sweet potato, peeled and grated

1 cup shredded cabbage

1 cup halved broccoli florets

1 cup halved cauliflower florets

10 cups vegetable stock

2 cups chopped romaine lettuce

1 cup ditalini

1 Heat oil in a large pot or Dutch oven over medium heat. Add leek, garlic, carrots, celery, bell pepper, bay leaves, and thyme. Season with ½ teaspoon salt and ¼ teaspoon black pepper. Cover and cook 10 minutes until vegetables are softened.

2 Add sweet potato and cook 2 minutes. Add cabbage, broccoli, and cauliflower. Cook another minute.

3 Add stock, increase heat to medium-high, and bring soup to a boil. Reduce heat to medium-low and cook 15 minutes. Add lettuce and pasta and cook another 20–25 minutes until pasta is tender.

4 Season with remaining ½ teaspoon salt and ¾ teaspoon black pepper. Remove and discard thyme sprigs and bay leaves. Serve hot.

Vegetarian Chili

Think of this as "chili con carne-ish." Lentils replace the meat in this warm and comforting bowl.

2 tablespoons extra-virgin olive oil

1 large yellow onion, peeled and chopped

1 small green bell pepper, seeded and chopped

1 small red bell pepper, seeded and chopped

3 cloves garlic, peeled and smashed

1 (28-ounce) can diced tomatoes

1 (15-ounce) can kidney beans, undrained

1 (15-ounce) can brown lentils, drained and rinsed

2 chipotle peppers in adobo sauce, chopped

1 bay leaf

3 tablespoons chili powder

1 teaspoon dried oregano

½ teaspoon salt

½ teaspoon ground black pepper

SERVES 6

Per Serving:

Calories	220
Fat	6g
Sodium	1,020mg
Carbohydrates	33g
Fiber	8g
Sugar	7g
Protein	10g

1 Heat oil in a large skillet over medium-high heat. Sauté onion and bell peppers 6–8 minutes until softened. Add garlic and sauté 1 minute.

2 Stir in tomatoes, beans, lentils, chipotle peppers, bay leaf, chili powder, oregano, salt, and black pepper. Bring to a boil, then reduce heat to medium-low.

3 Simmer 30–40 minutes until most of the liquid has been absorbed.

4 Remove and discard bay leaf before serving.

Fassoulada (Greek White Bean Soup)

SERVES 6

Per Serving:

Calories	140
Fat	11g
Sodium	550mg
Carbohydrates	15g
Fiber	2g
Sugar	3g
Protein	4g

This bean soup is a national dish in Greece—every home cook makes it. Although there are many regional twists to this hearty soup, the approach is the same—simple.

1 cup dried navy beans, soaked overnight in water to cover and drained

1 stalk celery, trimmed, halved lengthwise, and sliced

1 large carrot, peeled, halved horizontally, and diagonally sliced

2 medium yellow onions, peeled and diced

½ cup tomato purée

¼ cup extra-virgin olive oil

2 bay leaves

1 small Calabrian chili pepper, chopped

2 teaspoons smoked paprika

8 cups water

1 teaspoon salt

1 Place beans, celery, carrot, onions, tomato purée, oil, bay leaves, chili pepper, paprika, and water in a large stockpot and bring to a boil over high heat.

2 Reduce heat to medium-low, cover, and simmer 1½ hours. Remove and discard bay leaves. Season with salt.

3 Serve immediately.

Fakes (Greek Lentil Soup)

This popular soup is eaten all over Greece. Using humble ingredients, it's filling and full of protein and iron. Make it part of your regular rotation.

2 cups dried brown lentils, rinsed and picked through

2 tablespoons extra-virgin olive oil

2 medium yellow onions, peeled and diced

1 large carrot, peeled, halved horizontally, and sliced

1 medium red bell pepper, seeded and diced

¾ cup tomato sauce

3 cloves garlic, peeled and smashed

3 bay leaves

1 tablespoon paprika

¾ teaspoon salt

2 tablespoons dried oregano

5 cloves garlic, peeled and minced

2 tablespoons red wine vinegar

SERVES 6

Per Serving:

Calories	310
Fat	6g
Sodium	450mg
Carbohydrates	50g
Fiber	10g
Sugar	5g
Protein	17g

1 Place lentils in a large pot and cover with water. Bring to a boil over high heat. Boil 1 minute, then drain. Return lentils to pot, keeping the heat high.

2 Add oil, onions, carrot, bell pepper, tomato sauce, smashed garlic, bay leaves, paprika, salt, and 8 cups water. Bring to a boil.

3 Reduce heat to low, cover, and simmer 50 minutes or until lentils are tender. Remove and discard bay leaves. Stir in oregano and minced garlic.

4 Ladle into bowls and drizzle with vinegar before serving.

Yellow Split Pea Soup

SERVES 6

Per Serving:

Calories	280
Fat	1.5g
Sodium	220mg
Carbohydrates	52g
Fiber	20g
Sugar	4g
Protein	17g

If you want to add meat to the soup, simmer a large smoked turkey leg with the peas.

1 pound dried yellow split peas, rinsed and picked through

7 cups water

2 large carrots, peeled and thinly sliced

1 medium yellow onion, peeled and chopped

2 teaspoons smoked paprika

½ teaspoon ground allspice

1 bay leaf

½ teaspoon salt

½ teaspoon ground black pepper

1 Place peas, water, carrots, onion, paprika, allspice, and bay leaf in a large pot or Dutch oven. Bring to a boil over high heat. Reduce heat to medium-low, cover, and simmer 1 hour.

2 Remove and discard bay leaf. Use an immersion blender to purée the soup until almost smooth, or transfer in batches to a blender to purée.

3 Season with salt and pepper before serving.

Trahana Soup with Tomato and Feta

This thick and comforting soup is perfect for a blustery winter day.

2 tablespoons extra-virgin olive oil

½ cup minced yellow onion

1 cup sour trahana

4 cups vegetable stock

1 cup tomato purée

½ teaspoon salt

¼ teaspoon ground black pepper

½ cup low-fat milk

½ cup crumbled feta cheese

1 teaspoon minced fresh oregano or ½ teaspoon dried oregano

SERVES 4

Per Serving:

Calories	330
Fat	13g
Sodium	860mg
Carbohydrates	42g
Fiber	2g
Sugar	10g
Protein	10g

1 Heat oil in a medium saucepan over medium-high heat. Sauté onion 5 minutes.

2 Stir in trahana, stock, tomato purée, salt, and pepper. Bring to a boil. Reduce heat to medium-low and simmer uncovered 15 minutes, stirring occasionally.

3 Add milk and cook, stirring, 1 minute.

4 Before serving, top with feta and oregano.

Leek and Prune Stew

SERVES 4

Per Serving:

Calories	230
Fat	7g
Sodium	430mg
Carbohydrates	41g
Fiber	5g
Sugar	21g
Protein	3g

This combination of prunes and leeks is a nice balance of sweet and savory. Serve it with crusty whole-grain bread.

2 tablespoons extra-virgin olive oil

3 cups chopped leeks

16 pitted prunes

1 cup tomato purée

2 bay leaves

½ teaspoon salt

¼ teaspoon ground black pepper

2 tablespoons balsamic vinegar

1 Heat oil in a medium saucepan over medium-high heat. Add leeks and sauté 6–7 minutes until translucent.
2 Add prunes, tomato purée, bay leaves, salt, pepper, and just enough hot water to cover. Bring to a boil.
3 Reduce heat to low, cover, and simmer 30 minutes. Uncover and simmer 5 minutes.
4 Remove and discard bay leaves. Stir in vinegar before serving.

Mushroom Magheritsa Soup

Magheritsa is a traditional Easter soup traditionally eaten by Greeks after mass on Easter Saturday. Use any mushrooms you like—cremini, button, shiitake, or oyster—in this vegetarian version. Serve it with a wedge of lemon.

2 tablespoons extra-virgin olive oil

12 scallions, trimmed and sliced

½ head romaine lettuce, finely chopped

1½ pounds fresh mushrooms (any variety), sliced

1 teaspoon salt

½ teaspoon ground black pepper

12 cups vegetable stock

½ cup long-grain white rice

½ cup finely chopped fresh parsley

1 cup finely chopped fresh dill, divided

2 large eggs

2 tablespoons lemon juice

1 teaspoon cornstarch

SERVES 8

Per Serving:

Calories	150
Fat	5g
Sodium	710mg
Carbohydrates	22g
Fiber	2g
Sugar	7g
Protein	6g

EASY BLENDING

If you have an immersion blender, use it instead of a whisk as you add the egg mixture to the soup.

1 Heat oil in a large pot or Dutch oven over medium heat. Add scallions and sauté 10 minutes. Add lettuce, mushrooms, salt, and pepper and sauté 7–8 minutes until mushrooms release their liquid.

2 Add stock, rice, parsley, and ½ cup dill. Increase heat to high and bring to a boil. Reduce heat to medium-low, cover, and simmer 25–30 minutes until rice is tender.

3 In a medium bowl, whisk eggs, lemon juice, and cornstarch until frothy.

4 Ladle about ½ cup hot liquid from the pot into the bowl with the egg mixture, whisking constantly. Continue whisking and add another ½ cup hot liquid. Pour mixture into the pot and stir to combine.

5 Add remaining ½ cup dill and serve.

Roasted Tomato Soup with Bulgur

When tomatoes are roasted, they develop a mildly smoky flavor. The natural sugars intensify, adding complexity to this soup.

8 medium plum tomatoes, halved

2 tablespoons plus ½ cup extra-virgin olive oil, divided

1½ teaspoons salt, divided

1 tablespoon tomato paste

2 medium yellow onions, peeled and quartered

1 large carrot, peeled and chopped

1 stalk celery, chopped

3 cloves garlic, peeled and chopped

3 large Roasted Red Peppers (see recipe in Chapter 11), chopped

3 bay leaves

7 cups vegetable stock

½ teaspoon ground black pepper

½ cup coarse (#3) bulgur

¼ cup chopped fresh mint

¼ cup crumbled feta cheese

2 tablespoons chopped fresh chives

SERVES 8

Per Serving:

Calories	280
Fat	21g
Sodium	800mg
Carbohydrates	21g
Fiber	4g
Sugar	9g
Protein	4g

MAKE-AHEAD TIP

If you're making this soup ahead of time, cook the bulgur separately and add to the reheated soup when serving. Doing this keeps the bulgur from soaking up all the liquid in your soup.

1 Preheat oven to 350°F.

2 Place tomatoes cut side up in an 8" × 8" baking pan. Drizzle with 2 tablespoons oil and sprinkle with ½ teaspoon salt. Roast 40 minutes. Remove from oven and transfer to a large pot or Dutch oven.

3 Add tomato paste, onions, carrot, celery, garlic, Roasted Red Peppers, bay leaves, stock, and remaining ½ cup oil. Heat over medium-high heat until the mixture comes to a boil. Reduce heat to medium-low and stir in black pepper and remaining 1 teaspoon salt. Simmer 45 minutes until vegetables are tender. Remove from heat.

4 Remove and discard bay leaves. Use an immersion blender to purée the soup until smooth, or transfer in batches to a blender to purée.

5 Add bulgur and simmer over medium-low heat, stirring occasionally, 20 minutes.

6 Remove from heat and stir in mint. Serve topped with feta and chives.

Three Mushroom and Wild Rice Soup

SERVES 6

This vegan soup is cozy, hearty, and creamy—without any cream at all. Three different types of mushrooms add depth and richness.

Per Serving:

Calories	220
Fat	8g
Sodium	494mg
Carbohydrates	33g
Fiber	3g
Sugar	7g
Protein	7g

⅓ cup dried shiitake mushrooms

3 tablespoons olive oil, divided

8 ounces cremini mushrooms, sliced

1½ teaspoons salt, divided

½ teaspoon ground black pepper, divided

½ cup wild rice

1 large yellow onion, peeled and diced

1 stalk celery, trimmed and diced

1 pound button mushrooms, sliced

1 bay leaf

6 sprigs fresh thyme

1 ounce brandy

1 large potato, peeled and grated

6 cups vegetable stock

1. In a large bowl, place dried mushrooms and cover with 2 cups boiling water. Cover and set aside 30 minutes. Strain mushrooms, reserving soaking liquid. Roughly chop mushrooms and set aside.

2. Heat 1 tablespoon oil in a medium skillet over medium-high heat. Sauté cremini mushrooms 8 minutes or until lightly browned. Season with ¼ teaspoon each salt and pepper. Set aside.

3. Meanwhile, bring 2 cups water to a boil in a medium saucepan over high heat. Add rice and 1 teaspoon salt. Reduce heat to low, cover, and simmer 30 minutes. Drain and set aside.

4. Heat remaining 2 tablespoons oil in a large saucepan over medium heat. Add onion, celery, button and shiitake mushrooms, bay leaf, thyme, and ¼ teaspoon each salt and pepper.

5. Cook, stirring occasionally, 5–7 minutes until softened. Add brandy and cook 2 minutes. Stir in potato, reserved mushroom soaking liquid, and stock. Increase heat to high and bring to a boil. Reduce heat to medium-low and simmer uncovered 30 minutes.

6. Remove and discard bay leaf and thyme sprigs. Use an immersion blender or transfer in batches to a blender to purée.

7. Return soup to stovetop over medium heat and stir in reserved rice. Simmer 5–10 minutes until rice is warmed.

8. Top with sautéed cremini mushrooms before serving.

Psarosoupa (Greek-Style Fish Soup)

For a thicker soup, remove a few pieces of potatoes and carrots after they're cooked and mash them before returning them to the pot.

3 tablespoons extra-virgin olive oil

3 medium yellow onions, peeled and quartered

2 stalks celery, trimmed and diced

3 medium carrots, peeled and sliced

3 large potatoes, peeled and roughly chopped

1¼ teaspoons salt, divided

10 cups water

6 (5-ounce) cod, haddock, or halibut fillets

2 large eggs

2 tablespoons lemon juice

1 tablespoon cornstarch

½ teaspoon ground black pepper

SERVES 6	
Per Serving:	
Calories	360
Fat	10g
Sodium	820mg
Carbohydrates	40g
Fiber	5g
Sugar	5g
Protein	28g

1 Heat oil in a large pot or Dutch oven over medium heat. Sauté onions, celery, and carrots 10 minutes. Add potatoes, 1 teaspoon salt, and water. Increase heat to high and bring to a boil.

2 Reduce heat to medium-low, cover, and simmer 30 minutes.

3 Add fish and increase heat to medium-high. Bring just to a boil, then reduce heat to medium-low. Cover and simmer 15 minutes. Remove fish with a slotted spoon and keep warm.

4 In a large bowl, whisk together eggs, lemon juice, and cornstarch. Using a large ladle, slowly transfer about 1 cup of the hot stock to the egg mixture, whisking constantly. Repeat with another ladle of stock, then stir the mixture into the pot. Season with pepper and remaining ¼ teaspoon salt.

5 Cut fish into small pieces and carefully stir into the soup. Serve immediately.

Corn Chowder with Shrimp

SERVES 6

Per Serving:

Calories	250
Fat	10g
Sodium	430mg
Carbohydrates	34g
Fiber	3g
Sugar	12g
Protein	8g

This sweet and savory chowder packs a spicy kick from the seasoning. You may want to double this recipe!

2 tablespoons extra-virgin olive oil

1 cup diced yellow onion

1 stalk celery, trimmed and diced

1 medium red bell pepper, seeded and diced

1 large russet potato, peeled and grated

1 (5-ounce) can evaporated milk

2 cups whole milk

1 cup low-sodium chicken or vegetable stock

1 (8.75-ounce) can cream-style corn

1 cup fresh corn or frozen kernels

2 teaspoons Old Bay or Cajun seasoning

1 pound small shrimp, peeled and deveined

½ teaspoon paprika

¼ cup sliced scallions

1 Heat oil in a large pot or Dutch oven over medium-high heat. Sauté onion, celery, and bell pepper 5-6 minutes.

2 Add potato, evaporated milk, whole milk, stock, cream-style corn, corn kernels, and seasoning. Bring to a boil, then reduce heat to low. Simmer 30 minutes, stirring often.

3 Stir in shrimp and simmer 5 minutes.

4 Ladle into bowls and top with paprika and scallions before serving.

Turkey Avgolemono

Turkey is a good lower-calorie protein to use in soups. If you prefer, you can make this one with chicken breast instead.

10 cups low-sodium chicken or turkey broth

¼ cup finely diced celery

¼ cup finely diced carrot

¼ cup Arborio rice

2 large eggs

2 tablespoons lemon juice

½ teaspoon salt

½ teaspoon ground black pepper

3 cups chopped cooked turkey breast

1 cup thinly sliced kale

SERVES 8

Per Serving:

Calories	120
Fat	2g
Sodium	770mg
Carbohydrates	7g
Fiber	1g
Sugar	0g
Protein	18g

1 In a large stockpot over high heat, bring broth to a boil. Add celery, carrot, and rice. Boil 20 minutes, then remove from heat.

2 In a large bowl, whisk together eggs and lemon juice. Using a large ladle, slowly transfer about 1 cup of the hot broth to the egg mixture, whisking constantly. Repeat with another ladle of broth, then stir the mixture into the pot. Season with salt and pepper.

3 Stir in turkey and kale. Heat over medium heat, stirring occasionally, 5 minutes.

4 Serve immediately.

Zucchini and Ground Turkey Stew

SERVES 4

Per Serving:

Calories	340
Fat	16g
Sodium	640mg
Carbohydrates	29g
Fiber	6g
Sugar	15g
Protein	31g

Ground turkey is a good substitute for ground beef, especially in sauces and stews.

2 tablespoons extra-virgin olive oil

1½ cups diced yellow onions

3 cloves garlic, peeled and minced

1 pound lean ground turkey

½ teaspoon salt

½ teaspoon ground black pepper

¼ cup dry white wine

2 cups tomato purée

3 bay leaves

5 whole allspice berries

6 medium zucchini, trimmed and sliced 1" thick

1 cup water

1 Heat oil in a large skillet over medium-high heat. Sauté onion 5-7 minutes until translucent. Add garlic and sauté 1 minute.

2 Add turkey, salt, and pepper and cook, stirring constantly, 5 minutes or until meat is browned.

3 Stir in wine and cook 2 minutes. Add tomato purée, bay leaves, allspice berries, zucchini, and water. Bring to a boil. Reduce heat to medium-low, cover, and simmer 30 minutes.

4 Remove and discard bay leaves before serving.

CHAPTER 8

Rice and Whole Grains

Saffron Rice

Saffron is a powerful antioxidant (but an expensive one). A little goes a long way, giving your dishes a vibrant yellow color and unique taste.

ARBORIO

Arborio rice is a short-grain rice with a creamy texture. Most supermarkets now carry Arborio rice as well as a number of other varieties.

2 tablespoons extra-virgin olive oil

1 medium yellow onion, peeled and finely chopped

2 cups Arborio rice

¼ cup dry white wine

¼ teaspoon saffron threads

6 cups vegetable stock

¼ cup grated Parmesan cheese

½ teaspoon salt

¼ teaspoon ground black pepper

1 Heat oil in a large saucepan over medium heat. Sauté onion 5 minutes or until translucent.

2 Add rice and stir 2 minutes to toast. Add wine and saffron and simmer about 5 minutes until most of the wine has cooked down.

3 Add stock and increase heat to high. Bring to a boil. Reduce heat to low, cover, and simmer 15 minutes, stirring occasionally.

4 Remove lid. If most of the liquid is not absorbed, cook uncovered 5 minutes.

5 Stir in Parmesan, salt, and pepper. Serve immediately.

Easy Dolmades

If you enjoy stuffed grape leaves but hate to roll them up, this dish is for you! This shortcut recipe gives you all the flavors of dolmades in an easy-to-assemble casserole.

2 tablespoons extra-virgin olive oil

1 small yellow onion, peeled and diced

1 clove garlic, peeled and minced

1 cup long-grain and wild rice blend

¼ cup chopped fresh parsley

2 teaspoons minced fresh mint

4 tablespoons lemon juice, divided

2 tablespoons raisins

2 tablespoons pine nuts

6 grape leaves packed in brine, drained, rinsed, and sliced into thin ribbons

3 cups vegetable stock

¼ cup chopped fresh dill

¼ teaspoon salt

¼ teaspoon ground black pepper

SERVES 4

Per Serving:

Calories	280
Fat	10g
Sodium	890mg
Carbohydrates	44g
Fiber	2g
Sugar	7g
Protein	5g

1 Preheat oven to 400°F.

2 Heat oil in a large skillet over medium heat. Sauté onion 5–7 minutes until translucent. Add garlic and sauté 1 minute. Add rice and cook, stirring, 2 minutes.

3 Transfer rice mixture to a large baking dish. Stir in parsley, mint, 2 tablespoons lemon juice, raisins, pine nuts, grape leaves, and stock. Bake 35–40 minutes until all the liquid has been absorbed.

4 Fluff mixture with a fork and stir in dill, salt, and pepper. Sprinkle with remaining 2 tablespoons lemon juice before serving.

Spanakorizo with Green Olives and Feta

Per Serving:

Calories	160
Fat	6g
Sodium	490mg
Carbohydrates	25g
Fiber	3g
Sugar	2g
Protein	6g

BAKED RICE

You can cook this rice dish in the oven. After the spinach has wilted in the pot, pour the contents into a deep casserole dish. Stir in stock and 1/4 cup dill. Cover the dish with foil and bake at 375°F 30 minutes. After baking, continue with step 3.

Spanakorizo means "spinach with rice." This makes a great vegetarian meal.

2 tablespoons extra-virgin olive oil

1 medium yellow onion, peeled and diced

2 cloves garlic, peeled and minced

1 cup long-grain white rice

2 pounds fresh spinach, chopped

1½ cups vegetable stock

½ cup plus 1 tablespoon chopped fresh dill, divided

2 tablespoons lemon juice

¾ teaspoon salt

½ teaspoon ground black pepper

¼ cup crumbled feta cheese

¼ cup chopped green olives

1 Heat oil in a medium heavy-bottomed pot over medium heat. Add onion and garlic and sauté 5 minutes or until onion is softened.

2 Add rice and stir to coat each grain in oil. Add spinach in batches, stirring until each batch is wilted down before adding the next, until all spinach has been added. Add stock and ¼ cup dill. Cover and cook 20 minutes until most of the liquid is absorbed.

3 Add lemon juice, ¼ cup dill, salt, and pepper. Fluff rice and transfer to a serving platter. Top with feta, olives, and remaining 1 tablespoon dill. Serve immediately.

Rice with Fide Noodles

SERVES 4

Per Serving:

Calories	420
Fat	8g
Sodium	470mg
Carbohydrates	83g
Fiber	0g
Sugar	2g
Protein	6g

Fide noodles are thin noodles that are sold in nests, ready to be crushed into soup. If you can't find fide noodles, look for Mexican fideo or break up thin vermicelli noodles into bite-sized pieces.

2 tablespoons extra-virgin olive oil

¾ cup crushed fide noodles or broken vermicelli

1½ cups long-grain white rice

2½ cups vegetable stock

½ teaspoon salt

¼ teaspoon ground black pepper

1 Heat oil in a medium saucepan over medium heat. Add noodles and toast, stirring, 4 minutes.

2 Add rice, stock, salt, and pepper and bring to a boil over medium-high heat.

3 Reduce heat to low, cover, and simmer 16 minutes undisturbed. Remove from heat and set aside 6 minutes.

4 Uncover, fluff mixture with a fork, and serve.

Tomato Rice with Shrimp

In this simple dish, rice is cooked in a tomato sauce and topped with herbed shrimp and crumbles of feta cheese.

3 tablespoons extra-virgin olive oil, divided

½ cup finely diced yellow onion

2 cups Arborio rice

1 cup tomato purée

5½ cups vegetable stock

1 cup chopped fresh chives, divided

¾ teaspoon salt, divided

½ teaspoon ground black pepper, divided

1 pound large shrimp, peeled and deveined, tails on

1 tablespoon chopped fresh tarragon

½ cup crumbled feta cheese

SERVES 6

Per Serving:

Calories	410
Fat	11g
Sodium	1,160mg
Carbohydrates	61g
Fiber	4g
Sugar	6g
Protein	19g

1 Heat 2 tablespoons oil in a medium saucepan over medium-high heat. Sauté onion 5 minutes or until translucent.

2 Add rice and stir 2 minutes to toast. Add tomato purée and stock and bring to a boil. Reduce heat to medium-low, partially cover, and simmer 15 minutes, stirring occasionally.

3 Remove from heat and stir in ¾ cup chives, ½ teaspoon salt, and ¼ teaspoon pepper. Set aside and keep warm.

4 Heat remaining 1 tablespoon oil in a large nonstick skillet over medium-high heat. Add shrimp to skillet in a single layer. Sprinkle with remaining ¼ teaspoon each salt and pepper. Sauté shrimp about 1 minute per side until pink. Remove from heat and stir in tarragon.

5 Divide rice among six plates or bowls. Top with shrimp, feta, and remaining ¼ cup chives. Serve immediately.

Rice Salad

This salad is great to take to a potluck or picnic. The punch of kalamata olives really heightens this easy and inventive dish.

1 cup cold cooked white or brown rice

1 large carrot, peeled and grated

½ cup finely diced green bell pepper

½ cup finely diced red bell pepper

1 cup fresh or frozen green peas

½ cup sliced kalamata olives

3 scallions, trimmed and chopped

¼ cup extra-virgin olive oil

3 tablespoons lemon juice

1 tablespoon grated lemon zest

½ teaspoon salt

½ teaspoon ground black pepper

½ cup chopped fresh parsley

½ cup chopped fresh dill

SERVES 6

Per Serving:

Calories	190
Fat	13g
Sodium	420mg
Carbohydrates	17g
Fiber	3g
Sugar	3g
Protein	3g

1 Combine rice, carrot, bell peppers, peas, olives, and scallions in a large bowl. In a small bowl, whisk together oil, lemon juice, lemon zest, salt, and black pepper. Pour over rice mixture and toss to coat.

2 Stir in parsley and dill before serving.

Barley Risotto with Mushrooms

SERVES 4

Per Serving:

Calories	310
Fat	9g
Sodium	650mg
Carbohydrates	48g
Fiber	9g
Sugar	5g
Protein	8g

Barley is filling and loaded with fiber. It can also help to keep your blood sugar level steady.

2 tablespoons extra-virgin olive oil

½ cup diced yellow onion

1 clove garlic, peeled and minced

2 cups sliced white mushrooms

2 bay leaves

¼ teaspoon fresh thyme leaves

1 cup pearl barley

¼ cup dry white wine

4 cups hot vegetable stock

½ teaspoon salt

¼ teaspoon ground black pepper

¼ cup grated Parmesan cheese

1 Heat oil in a medium saucepan over medium heat. Sauté onion 5-7 minutes until translucent. Add garlic and sauté 1 minute.

2 Stir in mushrooms, bay leaves, and thyme and sauté 5 minutes. Add barley and wine. Cook, stirring constantly, until the liquid is absorbed, about 5 minutes.

3 Add 1 cup stock and cook 5 minutes more, stirring until absorbed. Repeat with remaining stock, 1 cup at a time. It should take about 20 minutes to incorporate all of the stock.

4 Remove and discard bay leaves. Season with salt and pepper.

5 Divide among four bowls or plates and top with Parmesan before serving.

Wheat Berries with Grilled Vegetables

Wheat berries are truly a whole grain—they consist of the entire edible part of wheat kernels. They're high in fiber, iron, and protein as well as magnesium and vitamin E, and low in calories and fat.

1 cup wheat berries, soaked overnight in water to cover

4 cups cold water

1 small zucchini, trimmed and sliced into rounds

1 small Japanese eggplant, trimmed and sliced into rounds

1 large yellow onion, peeled and cut into wedges

1 large red bell pepper, seeded and cut into quarters

2 tablespoons extra-virgin olive oil

¾ teaspoon salt, divided

1½ tablespoons lemon juice

¼ cup finely chopped fresh parsley

2 tablespoons chopped fresh mint

1 teaspoon dried oregano

¼ teaspoon ground black pepper

¼ cup crumbled feta cheese

SERVES 6

Per Serving:

Calories	210
Fat	7g
Sodium	360mg
Carbohydrates	32g
Fiber	8g
Sugar	5g
Protein	7g

1 Drain wheat berries and place in a large pot over high heat. Add cold water and bring to a boil. Reduce heat to medium-low and simmer uncovered 1 hour until tender. Drain and set aside to cool.

2 Preheat a charcoal or gas grill.

3 Brush zucchini, eggplant, onion, and bell pepper with oil and sprinkle with ½ teaspoon salt. Grill 6–8 minutes, turning often, until slightly charred and tender. Remove from grill and roughly chop. Transfer to a large bowl.

4 Add wheat berries, lemon juice, parsley, mint, oregano, black pepper, and remaining ¼ teaspoon salt. Toss to combine.

5 Top with feta and serve.

Farro with Steamed Mussels

SERVES 4

Per Serving:

Calories	390
Fat	11g
Sodium	1,060mg
Carbohydrates	35g
Fiber	4g
Sugar	4g
Protein	33g

FARRO

Farro is a nutrient-packed grain with a nutty flavor. It can be used in place of rice in many recipes.

Mussels are delicious, affordable, and found at most seafood shops. They are rich in omega-3 fatty acids and provide all the protein of red meat without the fat.

¾ cup farro

½ teaspoon salt, divided

3 cups water

2 tablespoons extra-virgin olive oil

½ cup diced yellow onion

2 cloves garlic, peeled and minced

½ cup diced fennel

1 cup diced tomato

⅛ teaspoon crushed red pepper flakes

½ cup dry white wine

2 pounds fresh mussels, scrubbed and rinsed

½ teaspoon ground black pepper

¼ cup chopped fresh parsley

1 In a medium saucepan over high heat, place farro, ¼ teaspoon salt, and water. Bring to a boil. Reduce heat to medium-low, cover, and simmer 30 minutes.

2 Heat oil in a large stockpot over medium-high heat. Sauté onion, garlic, and fennel 5 minutes. Add tomato, red pepper flakes, and wine. Cook 5–6 minutes until sauce has thickened.

3 Add farro and mussels, cover, and cook another 5–6 minutes until mussels have opened. Discard any mussels that do not open.

4 Season with remaining ¼ teaspoon salt and pepper, top with parsley, and serve.

Lentil and Bulgur Salad with Walnuts

This salad is full of iron and fiber. Make it ahead of time and let the flavors marry and intensify overnight in the refrigerator. It makes a good base for a baked fish fillet.

¾ cup fine bulgur

¾ teaspoon salt, divided

1½ cups water

1 (15-ounce) can green lentils, drained and rinsed

1 cup diced red bell pepper

½ cup diced celery

1 cup thinly sliced scallions

1 cup roughly chopped walnuts

3 tablespoons lemon juice

1 tablespoon grated lemon zest

1 clove garlic, peeled and minced

1 teaspoon Dijon mustard

¼ cup extra-virgin olive oil

¼ teaspoon ground black pepper

SERVES 4

Per Serving:

Calories	500
Fat	34g
Sodium	610mg
Carbohydrates	43g
Fiber	7g
Sugar	3g
Protein	14g

1 Place bulgur and ¼ teaspoon salt in a medium saucepan and add water. Bring to a boil over high heat. Reduce heat to medium-low, cover, and simmer 8 minutes. Remove from heat, fluff with a fork, and set aside to cool 15 minutes.

2 In a large bowl, combine bulgur, lentils, bell pepper, celery, scallions, and walnuts.

3 In a small bowl, whisk together lemon juice, lemon zest, garlic, mustard, oil, black pepper, and remaining ½ teaspoon salt. Pour over salad and toss to coat.

4 Serve at room temperature or refrigerate at least 2 hours before serving.

Spanish-Style Saffron Quinoa

This fragrant dish goes well with grilled chicken or fish and looks very festive alongside shish kebabs. Use saffron threads instead of powder, if possible.

2 tablespoons extra-virgin olive oil

1 medium yellow onion, peeled and thinly sliced

4 stalks celery, thinly sliced

3 medium tomatoes, cored and chopped

4 cups water

1 teaspoon salt

¼ teaspoon cayenne pepper

1⅓ cups quinoa

½ teaspoon saffron threads

1 Spray a 4- to 5-quart slow cooker with nonstick cooking spray.

2 Heat oil in a medium skillet over medium heat. Sauté onion and celery until softened, about 5–7 minutes. Transfer to slow cooker.

3 Add tomatoes, water, salt, and cayenne pepper to slow cooker. Cover and cook on low 4 hours.

4 Increase heat to high and add quinoa and saffron. Cover and cook 1 hour or until quinoa is tender.

SERVES 8

Per Serving:

Calories	150
Fat	5g
Sodium	320mg
Carbohydrates	22g
Fiber	3g
Sugar	3g
Protein	5g

SAFFRON

Saffron is a spice derived from the dried stigmas of crocus plants. The crocus must be picked by hand so that the delicate stigmas are kept intact. Because of this, saffron is the most expensive spice in the world. Thankfully, a little goes a long way to add rich flavor and bright color to a dish.

Quinoa Tabbouleh Salad

SERVES 4

Per Serving:

Calories	130
Fat	4.5g
Sodium	220mg
Carbohydrates	18g
Fiber	2g
Sugar	2g
Protein	4g

Tabbouleh is usually made with bulgur wheat, but this high-protein version uses quinoa. Swap out the white beans for black beans, chickpeas, or lentils, if you prefer.

1 cup cooked quinoa

2½ tablespoons lemon juice

2 teaspoons grated lemon zest

½ cup thinly sliced scallions

1 clove garlic, peeled and minced

1 tablespoon extra-virgin olive oil

½ cup canned white beans, drained and rinsed

½ cup finely chopped parsley

2 tablespoons chopped fresh mint

½ cup diced cucumber

½ cup diced tomatoes

¼ teaspoon salt

⅛ teaspoon ground black pepper

1 In a large bowl, combine quinoa, lemon juice, lemon zest, scallions, and garlic. Cover and refrigerate 30 minutes.

2 Stir in oil, beans, parsley, mint, cucumber, tomato, salt, and pepper. Serve immediately or refrigerate at least 2 hours before serving.

Smoked Popcorn

MAKES 8 CUPS

Per Serving (2 cups):

Calories	90
Fat	7g
Sodium	290mg
Carbohydrates	0g
Fiber	0g
Sugar	0g
Protein	1g

Skip the butter and try olive oil with your popcorn. You can also use this recipe as a base for popcorn and shake it up with other flavors like herbs or other spices.

¼ cup popcorn kernels

2 tablespoons extra-virgin olive oil

½ teaspoon salt

¼ teaspoon smoked paprika

1 Place popcorn, oil, and salt in a medium covered saucepan over medium heat. Shake pan occasionally as corn kernels pop. Remove from heat when the popping slows.

2 Transfer popcorn to a large bowl and sprinkle with paprika. Toss to coat and serve.

CHAPTER 9

Pasta

Spaghetti with Tomato and Basil

SERVES 6

Per Serving:

Calories	320
Fat	10g
Sodium	542mg
Carbohydrates	48g
Fiber	2g
Sugar	5g
Protein	11g

This pasta dish tastes like summer in a bowl. Use ripe summer tomatoes and fresh basil from the garden for best results.

3 tablespoons extra-virgin olive oil, divided

4 cloves garlic, peeled and minced

1 (28-ounce) can whole tomatoes, hand crushed

½ teaspoon ground black pepper

3½ teaspoons salt, divided

12 ounces whole-wheat spaghetti

1 cup sliced fresh basil

4 tablespoons grated Romano cheese, divided

1 In a large skillet over medium heat, heat 2 tablespoons oil 30 seconds. Add garlic and cook 2 minutes until fragrant. Add tomatoes (including liquid) and increase heat to medium-high. Bring to a boil, then reduce heat to medium-low. Stir in pepper and ½ teaspoon salt and cook 10–12 minutes until thickened.

2 Meanwhile, fill a large pot two-thirds with water and place over medium-high heat. Add remaining 3 teaspoons salt and bring to a boil. Add pasta and cook about 6–7 minutes until al dente. Reserve ¼ cup pasta-cooking water and drain pasta.

3 Add pasta to sauce and stir to combine. If sauce is a little thin or dry, stir in reserved pasta water. Add basil and stir to combine.

4 Add 2 tablespoons Romano and toss to combine.

5 Top pasta with remaining 2 tablespoons Romano and drizzle with remaining 1 tablespoon oil. Serve hot.

Penne all'Arrabbiata

This dish is zesty from the crushed red pepper flakes and gooey from the melted mozzarella. It is a quick and easy dinner to pull together.

2 tablespoons extra-virgin olive oil

1 medium yellow onion, peeled and diced

6 cloves garlic, peeled and minced

2 cups canned whole tomatoes, hand crushed

½ teaspoon ground black pepper

3½ teaspoons salt, divided

12 ounces whole-wheat penne rigate

1 cup shredded mozzarella cheese

1 teaspoon crushed red pepper flakes

1 cup torn fresh basil

½ cup grated Romano or Parmesan cheese

1 Heat oil in a large skillet over medium heat. Sauté onion and garlic 5 minutes until onion is softened. Add tomatoes, black pepper, and ½ teaspoon salt. Cook 20 minutes or until sauce has thickened.

2 Meanwhile, fill a large pot two-thirds with water and place over medium-high heat. Add remaining 3 teaspoons salt and bring to a boil. Add pasta and cook 8–9 minutes until al dente. Reserve ¼ cup pasta-cooking water and drain pasta.

3 Add pasta to sauce and stir to combine. If sauce is a little thin or dry, stir in reserved pasta water. Add mozzarella, red pepper flakes, and basil. Stir until mozzarella has melted.

4 Top with Romano and serve.

SERVES 6

Per Serving:

Calories	370
Fat	15g
Sodium	662mg
Carbohydrates	43g
Fiber	2g
Sugar	6g
Protein	20g

PENNE RIGATE

Penne rigate is a short, thick, ridged, hollow pasta. It is perfect for a thick tomato sauce because the sauce sticks to the outside ridges and fills the inside. Every bite is a burst of flavor!

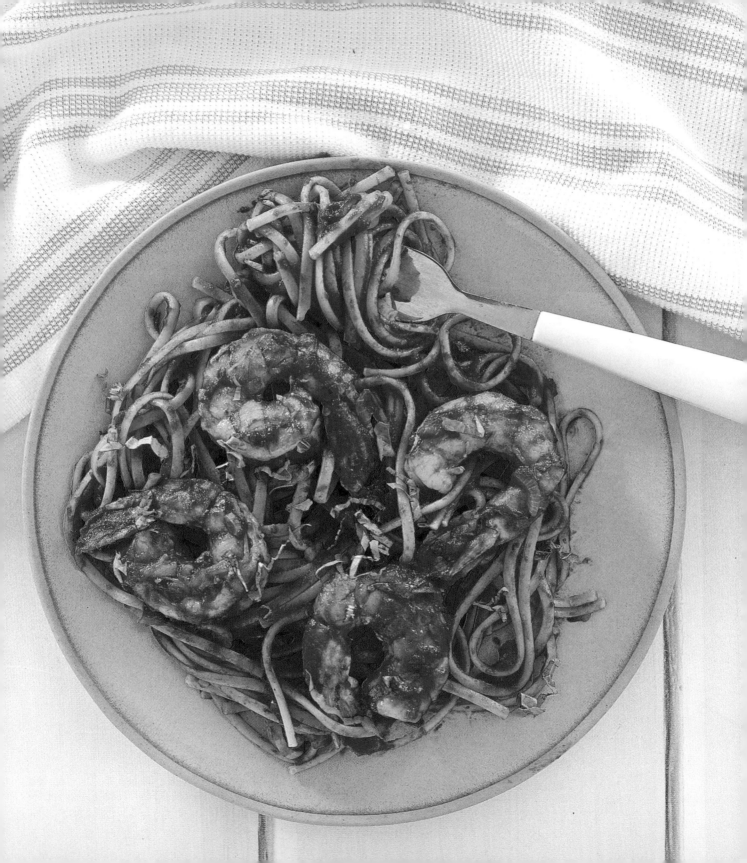

Mediterranean Shrimp and Pasta

This recipe can be easily doubled to serve twelve or increased even more for larger numbers of hungry guests.

3½ teaspoons salt, divided

12 ounces whole-wheat linguine

24 medium shrimp, peeled, deveined, and shells reserved

¼ teaspoon ground black pepper

⅓ cup extra-virgin olive oil

1 medium onion, peeled and finely chopped

4 cloves garlic, peeled and minced

¼ cup dry white wine

2 cups tomato purée

¼ teaspoon crushed red pepper flakes

½ cup chopped fresh parsley

¼ cup chopped fresh basil

SERVES 6

Per Serving:

Calories	390
Fat	16g
Sodium	592mg
Carbohydrates	47g
Fiber	2g
Sugar	8g
Protein	14g

1 Fill a large pot two-thirds with water and place over medium-high heat. Add 3 teaspoons salt and bring to a boil. Add pasta and cook 6–7 minutes until al dente. Drain pasta and keep warm.

2 Wrap shrimp shells in cheesecloth and use twine to tie it up tightly into a bundle. Set aside. Season shrimp with black pepper and ¼ teaspoon salt.

3 Heat oil in a large skillet over medium-high heat 30 seconds. Add shrimp and cook 1 minute on each side until pink. Remove shrimp, leaving oil in skillet, and set aside.

4 Reduce heat to medium and add onion, garlic, and shrimp shells in cheesecloth. Cook 5 minutes until onion is softened. Add wine and cook 5 minutes.

5 Add tomato purée, increase heat to medium-high, and bring sauce to a boil. Decrease heat to medium and cook 20 minutes until sauce thickens. Remove shrimp shells and discard.

6 Add pasta to skillet and toss to coat. Remove skillet from heat and add cooked shrimp, red pepper flakes, parsley, remaining ¼ teaspoon salt, and basil. Toss to combine the ingredients and serve immediately.

CRUSHED RED PEPPER FLAKES

Crushed red pepper flakes are made from hot peppers that are dried and crushed. Most crushed red pepper flakes include the seeds, which are the hottest part of the pepper. Depending on the peppers used, some brands are hotter than others. Be careful when you first use them. Add only a little at a time to make sure the dish is not too hot for your taste. You can always add more heat, but you can't take it away.

Spaghetti with Brown Butter and Feta

SERVES 4

Per Serving:

Calories	430
Fat	26g
Sodium	298mg
Carbohydrates	42g
Fiber	0g
Sugar	2g
Protein	10g

Brown butter has a lovely nutty taste. This recipe can be easily doubled or tripled.

2¼ teaspoons salt, divided

8 ounces whole-wheat spaghetti

¼ cup unsalted butter

3 tablespoons extra-virgin olive oil, divided

2 cloves garlic, peeled and smashed

2 tablespoons grated kefalotyri or Romano cheese

2 tablespoons crumbled feta cheese, divided

¼ teaspoon ground black pepper

1 Fill a large pot two-thirds with water and place over medium-high heat. Add 2 teaspoons salt and bring to a boil. Add pasta and cook 6–7 minutes until al dente. Drain pasta and keep warm.

2 Melt butter in a large skillet over medium heat. Add 2 tablespoons oil and garlic. Whisk constantly 1–2 minutes until butter turns a chestnut-brown color. Remove from heat and cool slightly. Remove and discard garlic.

3 Add pasta to brown butter and stir to combine. Add kefalotyri and 1 tablespoon feta and continue to toss until cheeses have blended in with butter. Season with pepper and remaining ¼ teaspoon salt.

4 Serve pasta topped with remaining 1 tablespoon feta and drizzled with remaining 1 tablespoon oil.

Makaronia with Tarama

Tarama is fish roe and can be found at Greek or Middle Eastern grocery stores. The Greek word makaronia *encompasses all varieties of pasta. Spaghetti is one type of* makaronia.

1 tablespoon salt

1 pound whole-wheat spaghetti

⅓ cup extra-virgin olive oil

1 cup coarse plain bread crumbs

¼ cup finely chopped blanched almonds

1 ounce ouzo

4 tablespoons tarama (fish roe)

2 cloves garlic, peeled and minced

¼ cup chopped fresh parsley

½ cup chopped scallions

2 tablespoons grated lemon zest

1 teaspoon dried oregano

1 tablespoon lemon juice

¼ teaspoon crushed red pepper flakes

SERVES 8

Per Serving:

Calories	380
Fat	19g
Sodium	232mg
Carbohydrates	55g
Fiber	1g
Sugar	4g
Protein	12g

1 Fill a large pot two-thirds with water and place over medium-high heat. Add salt and bring to a boil. Add pasta and cook 6–7 minutes until al dente. Drain pasta and keep warm.

2 Heat oil in a large skillet over medium heat. Add bread crumbs and almonds and cook, stirring constantly, 2 minutes until lightly browned. Add ouzo, tarama, and garlic and cook another 2 minutes until ouzo is absorbed.

3 Remove from heat and add parsley, scallions, lemon zest, and oregano. Add pasta to skillet. Toss to combine and to coat pasta.

4 Add lemon juice and red pepper flakes and toss to combine. Serve immediately.

Linguine with Tapenade

SERVES 8

Per Serving:

Calories	380
Fat	32g
Sodium	680mg
Carbohydrates	24g
Fiber	3g
Sugar	2g
Protein	5g

For a variation, serve this delicious tapenade on its own as you might with any sauce, or use it as a topping on toast.

1 cup oil-cured pitted ripe olives

2 tablespoons drained and rinsed capers

1½ tablespoons fresh rosemary leaves

1 clove garlic, peeled and smashed

2 oil-packed anchovy fillets, drained

½ teaspoon sugar

⅔ cup plus 2 tablespoons extra-virgin olive oil, divided

1 pound whole-wheat linguine, cooked al dente and drained

¼ cup grated pecorino Romano cheese

1 tablespoon chopped fresh chives

1 Place olives, capers, rosemary, garlic, anchovies, sugar, and ⅔ cup oil in a food processor. Process until mixture is well incorporated but not smooth. The tapenade should still have texture.

2 Toss pasta with remaining 2 tablespoons oil and pecorino Romano. Arrange pasta on a serving platter and top it with tapenade and chives.

Shrimp, Macaroni, and Feta

This dish is part shrimp saganaki and part macaroni and cheese.

SERVES 12

Per Serving:

Calories	290
Fat	14g
Sodium	360mg
Carbohydrates	30g
Fiber	1g
Sugar	6g
Protein	11g

3½ teaspoons salt, divided

2½ cups whole-wheat elbow macaroni

2 large red serrano chili peppers, seeded and chopped

2 whole cloves garlic

¼ cup chopped fresh parsley

1¼ cups sliced fresh basil, divided

6 tablespoons olive oil, divided

½ teaspoon honey

2 tablespoons lemon juice

1 small red onion, peeled and finely chopped

1 clove garlic, peeled and minced

1 teaspoon paprika

1 cup sliced button mushrooms

6 medium plum tomatoes, cored, peeled, and puréed

¼ teaspoon ground black pepper

¼ cup dry white wine

1 ounce ouzo

1 cup evaporated milk

1½ cups crumbled feta cheese, divided

24 medium shrimp, peeled and deveined

1 teaspoon dried oregano

1 Fill a large pot two-thirds with water and place over medium-high heat. Add 3 teaspoons salt and bring water to a boil. Add pasta and cook 6–7 minutes until al dente. Drain pasta and keep warm.

2 Preheat broiler.

3 In a food processor, place chilies, whole garlic, parsley, ¼ cup basil, 4 tablespoons oil, honey, lemon juice, and ¼ teaspoon salt. Pulse until incorporated. Set aside.

4 In a skillet over medium heat, heat remaining 2 tablespoons oil. Add onion, minced garlic, paprika, and mushrooms. Cook 5 minutes until onion is softened. Add tomatoes and season with pepper and remaining ¼ teaspoon salt. Simmer 5–7 minutes until slightly thickened. Add wine and ouzo and cook 5 minutes until most liquid has evaporated.

5 Add milk and 1 cup feta and cook 3 minutes until sauce is thickened. Stir in pasta and remaining 1 cup basil. Toss to combine.

6 Pour pasta into a medium baking dish and top with shrimp and remaining ½ cup feta. Broil 5 minutes until shrimp turn pink and cheese is melted. Drizzle with parsley sauce and sprinkle with oregano. Cool 5 minutes before serving.

Spaghetti with Mussels, Parsley, and Lemon

Try using fresh clams or shrimp in place of mussels in this dish.

3 tablespoons extra-virgin olive oil

8 cloves garlic, peeled and thinly sliced

3 pounds fresh mussels, scrubbed and rinsed

¼ cup plus 2 tablespoons chopped fresh parsley, divided

½ cup dry white wine

¼ cup lemon juice

1 pound whole-wheat spaghetti, cooked and drained

1½ teaspoons grated lemon zest

½ teaspoon crushed red pepper flakes

½ teaspoon salt

1 Heat oil in a large skillet over medium-high heat. Add garlic and cook 1 minute or until lightly browned. Add mussels and ¼ cup parsley. Cook 2 minutes while stirring. Add wine and cook another 2 minutes. Add lemon juice and cover the skillet. Cook 4–5 minutes until mussels open. Uncover skillet and discard any unopened mussels.

2 Add pasta, lemon zest, red pepper flakes, and salt to the mussels. Toss to combine the ingredients and to coat the pasta. Sprinkle with remaining 2 tablespoons parsley and serve immediately.

SERVES 8

Per Serving:

Calories	160
Fat	6g
Sodium	180mg
Carbohydrates	19g
Fiber	2g
Sugar	1g
Protein	5g

AL DENTE

Al dente means "to the tooth" in Italian. It refers to pasta that is cooked but not soft. The cooked pasta should be slightly firm and still hold its shape. Perfectly cooked pasta is the best vehicle for a delicious sauce.

Garidomakaronada with Ouzo and Fresh Tomatoes

Garidomakaronada *is a compound word in Greek meaning "pasta and shrimp." The long, thick, hollow shape of bucatini allows this aromatic seafood sauce to get right into the pasta.*

SERVES 8

Per Serving:

Calories	310
Fat	9g
Sodium	302mg
Carbohydrates	50g
Fiber	2g
Sugar	7g
Protein	11g

16 medium shrimp, peeled and deveined

3½ teaspoons salt, divided

½ teaspoon ground black pepper, divided

¼ cup extra-virgin olive oil

1 large yellow onion, peeled and finely chopped

3 cloves garlic, peeled and smashed

4 large, very ripe tomatoes, cored, peeled, and puréed

1½ tablespoons tomato paste

1 ounce ouzo

1 pound whole-wheat bucatini

½ teaspoon crushed red pepper flakes

2 tablespoons chopped fresh parsley

1 Season shrimp with ¼ teaspoon salt and ¼ teaspoon black pepper. Heat oil in a large skillet over medium-high heat. Add shrimp and cook 1 minute on each side until pink. Remove shrimp from skillet, leaving the oil in the skillet, and reserve.

2 Reduce heat to medium and add onion and garlic. Cook 5 minutes until onion is softened. Add puréed tomatoes and tomato paste. Increase heat to high and bring to a boil. Reduce heat to medium-low and cook 15–20 minutes until thickened. Stir in ouzo, ¼ teaspoon salt, and remaining ¼ teaspoon black pepper.

3 Meanwhile, fill a large pot two-thirds with water and place over medium-high heat. Add remaining 3 teaspoons salt and bring to a boil. Add pasta and cook 6–7 minutes until al dente. Drain pasta and add to sauce along with red pepper flakes and cooked shrimp. Remove from heat and toss to coat the pasta.

4 Sprinkle with parsley and serve immediately.

Seven-Ingredient Anchovy Fusilli

This simple pasta is surprisingly rich and so easy to make. Despite using a slow cooker, it's done in only 45 minutes.

1 pound whole-wheat fusilli

4 (15-ounce) cans low-sodium chicken broth

1 (10-ounce) can oil-packed anchovies, drained and chopped

¼ cup extra-virgin olive oil

1 clove garlic, peeled and minced

¼ cup chopped fresh parsley

½ teaspoon salt

SERVES 8

Per Serving:

Calories	360
Fat	11g
Sodium	1,510mg
Carbohydrates	45g
Fiber	0g
Sugar	3g
Protein	18g

1 Place pasta and broth in a 6-quart slow cooker. Cook on high 30 minutes, check for doneness, and cook an additional 15 minutes if needed.

2 Stir in anchovies, oil, and garlic. Sprinkle with parsley and salt. Remove from heat and serve.

Garlic and Artichoke Pasta

SERVES 6

Per Serving:

Calories	230
Fat	4g
Sodium	760mg
Carbohydrates	39g
Fiber	6g
Sugar	10g
Protein	11g

Artichoke hearts give this sauce a unique and savory flavor that is perfect for pasta or rice.

2 (14.5-ounce) cans diced tomatoes with basil, oregano, and garlic

2 (14-ounce) cans artichoke hearts, drained and quartered

6 cloves garlic, peeled and minced

½ cup evaporated milk

12 ounces whole-wheat ziti, cooked al dente and drained

1 Add tomatoes, artichokes, and garlic to a 4- to 5-quart slow cooker. Cook on high 3 hours or on low 6 hours.

2 Twenty minutes prior to serving, stir in milk. Serve over pasta.

Spaghetti with Roasted Cherry Tomatoes and Basil

Cherry tomatoes can be counted on to be sweet and flavorful all year round. They're your best bet when tomatoes are not in season.

2 cups cherry tomatoes

2 tablespoons extra-virgin olive oil

3½ teaspoons salt, divided

4 ounces whole-wheat spaghetti

3 cloves garlic, peeled and minced

1 cup thinly sliced fresh basil

¼ teaspoon ground black pepper

¼ cup grated Parmesan cheese

1　Preheat oven to 450°F.

2　Place tomatoes in a medium oven-safe skillet. Drizzle with oil, sprinkle with ½ teaspoon salt, and toss. Roast tomatoes 30–40 minutes until they are shriveled and beginning to brown.

3　Fill a large pot two-thirds with water and place over high heat. Add remaining 3 teaspoons salt and bring to a boil. Add pasta and cook 7–8 minutes until al dente. Reserve 1 cup pasta-cooking water and drain pasta.

4　Place skillet with tomatoes over medium heat. Add reserved pasta water and stir to deglaze the pan. Add garlic and cook 1 minute.

5　Add pasta to skillet and toss to combine. Top with basil, pepper, and Parmesan. Serve immediately.

SERVES 2

Per Serving:

Calories	410
Fat	19g
Sodium	842mg
Carbohydrates	51g
Fiber	2g
Sugar	6g
Protein	13g

Pasta Salad with Feta, Sun-Dried Tomatoes, and Spinach

SERVES 8

Per Serving:

Calories	210
Fat	15g
Sodium	482mg
Carbohydrates	15g
Fiber	1g
Sugar	2g
Protein	7g

Pasta salads are great for backyard entertaining, picnics, or potluck dinners. Use bow tie pasta because it makes it easy to grab a forkful of all the ingredients with one stab.

3½ teaspoons salt, divided

1½ cups whole-wheat farfalle (bow tie pasta)

1 cup chopped baby spinach

8 oil-packed sun-dried tomatoes, sliced

1 cup grated carrots

2 scallions, trimmed and thinly sliced

1 clove garlic, peeled and minced

1 medium dill pickle, diced

⅓ cup extra-virgin olive oil

2 tablespoons red wine vinegar

½ cup plain low-fat Greek yogurt

½ teaspoon ground black pepper

1 teaspoon chopped fresh oregano

¼ cup chopped fresh basil

1 cup diced feta cheese

¼ cup chopped fresh chives

1 Fill a large pot two-thirds with water and place over medium-high heat. Add 3 teaspoons salt and bring to a boil. Add pasta and cook 6–7 minutes until al dente. Drain pasta in a colander and cool it under cold running water.

2 In a large bowl, combine spinach, tomatoes, carrots, scallions, garlic, and pickle. Add pasta and toss to combine.

3 In a medium bowl, whisk oil, vinegar, yogurt, pepper, and remaining ½ teaspoon salt. Add dressing to pasta and toss to combine and coat evenly. Toss in oregano, basil, and feta.

4 Sprinkle salad with chives. Refrigerate until cold or serve at room temperature.

Greek-Style Rigatoni

Capers make a good addition to this dish.

⅓ cup extra-virgin olive oil

8 ounces whole-wheat rigatoni, cooked al dente and drained

6 ounces feta cheese, cubed

½ cup chopped kalamata olives

10 oil-packed sun-dried tomatoes, drained and sliced

1 tablespoon dried oregano

1 teaspoon ground black pepper

1 Heat oil in large sauté pan over medium heat. Add pasta, feta, olives, and tomatoes. Toss mixture to combine and cook 2–3 minutes until cheese just starts to melt.

2 Season with oregano and pepper. Serve hot.

SERVES 6

Per Serving:

Calories	293
Fat	23g
Sodium	487mg
Carbohydrates	16g
Fiber	2g
Sugar	1g
Protein	7g

Herb and Lemon Couscous

Change up the herbs and use whatever you have on hand. Serve this side with fish or chicken.

2¼ cups water

½ teaspoon salt

2 teaspoons grated lemon zest

1 tablespoon lemon juice

2 tablespoons extra-virgin olive oil, divided

1½ cups couscous

1 tablespoon minced fresh parsley

1 tablespoon minced fresh chives

1 tablespoon minced fresh mint

SERVES 6

Per Serving:

Calories	210
Fat	5g
Sodium	200mg
Carbohydrates	34g
Fiber	2g
Sugar	0g
Protein	6g

1 In a medium pot over medium-high heat, combine water, salt, lemon zest, lemon juice, and 1 tablespoon oil. Bring to a boil and remove from heat. Stir in couscous. Cover and let stand 5 minutes until all liquid has been absorbed.

2 Fluff couscous with a fork. Stir in parsley, chives, mint, and remaining 1 tablespoon oil. Serve hot or at room temperature.

Saffron Couscous

SERVES 6

Per Serving:

Calories	200
Fat	4g
Sodium	200mg
Carbohydrates	34g
Fiber	2g
Sugar	0g
Protein	6g

This bright yellow dish is a delicious side for fish or seafood. Add some chopped grilled vegetables to the couscous and you have a fantastic vegetarian main dish.

2¼ cups water
½ teaspoon salt
⅛ teaspoon saffron threads
2 tablespoons unsalted butter, divided
1½ cups couscous

1 In a medium pot over medium-high heat, combine water, salt, saffron, and 1 tablespoon butter. Bring to a boil and remove from heat. Stir in couscous. Cover and let couscous stand 5 minutes until all liquid has been absorbed.

2 Fluff couscous with a fork and stir in remaining 1 tablespoon butter. Serve hot or at room temperature.

CHAPTER 10

Simple Poultry and Seafood Meals

White Beans and Turkey Sausage

SERVES 6

Per Serving:

Calories	340
Fat	8g
Sodium	910mg
Carbohydrates	44g
Fiber	3g
Sugar	6g
Protein	20g

A small serving of turkey sausage can go a long way in making you feel full and satisfied.

2 tablespoons extra-virgin olive oil

3 (3-ounce) Italian-style turkey sausages, cut in half crosswise

1 medium yellow onion, peeled and sliced

3 cloves garlic, peeled and minced

3 (15-ounce) cans cannellini beans, drained and rinsed

1 (28-ounce) can plum tomatoes, hand crushed

½ teaspoon smoked paprika

3 bay leaves

6 sprigs fresh thyme

1 teaspoon salt

½ teaspoon ground black pepper

3 cups baby spinach

1 Heat oil in a large skillet over medium-high heat. Add sausages and cook, turning often, 4–5 minutes until browned.

2 Add onion and garlic. Cook, stirring occasionally, 5 minutes. Stir in beans, tomatoes, paprika, bay leaves, thyme, salt, and pepper. Pour in enough water to just cover the contents of the skillet. Bring to a low boil.

3 Reduce heat to medium-low, cover, and simmer 30 minutes, stirring occasionally.

4 Remove and discard bay leaves and thyme sprigs. Add spinach. Cook about 5 minutes until wilted.

5 Serve immediately.

Turkey Chili

This chili is thick and hearty and bursting with flavor. It can also be made with cubes of leftover turkey.

1 tablespoon extra-virgin olive oil

1 pound lean ground turkey

½ teaspoon salt

½ teaspoon ground black pepper

1 large yellow onion, peeled and chopped

1 small green bell pepper, seeded and chopped

1 small red bell pepper, seeded and chopped

3 cloves garlic, peeled and smashed

1 bay leaf

1 (28-ounce) can diced tomatoes

3 tablespoons chili powder

1 (15-ounce) can red kidney beans, undrained

1 teaspoon dried oregano

2 chipotle peppers in adobo sauce, chopped

SERVES 6

Per Serving:

Calories	260
Fat	9g
Sodium	920mg
Carbohydrates	26g
Fiber	9g
Sugar	7g
Protein	23g

1 Heat oil in a large pot or Dutch oven over medium-high heat. Add turkey and sauté until no longer pink, about 5 minutes. Season with salt and black pepper.

2 Add onion, bell peppers, garlic, and bay leaf. Sauté 10 minutes. Stir in tomatoes, chili powder, beans, oregano, and chipotle peppers.

3 Bring to a boil, then reduce heat to medium-low. Simmer 30–40 minutes until most of the liquid has been absorbed and the chili is thick. Remove and discard bay leaf. Serve hot.

Chicken Meatballs with Mushrooms

SERVES 8

Per Serving:

Calories	280
Fat	14g
Sodium	440mg
Carbohydrates	12g
Fiber	1g
Sugar	4g
Protein	25g

CLEANING MUSHROOMS

It's best to avoid water when cleaning mushrooms. They will absorb the moisture, and waterlogged mushrooms will resist browning. All you need is a dry paper towel or soft brush to get the dirt off.

Ground chicken is a wonderful alternative to red meat. Make a batch of these meatballs for your family and they won't even know you're serving them chicken. Serve on a bed of rice or Dairy-Free Mashed Potatoes (see recipe in Chapter 11).

2 (1-ounce) slices stale whole-wheat bread

2 pounds ground chicken

1 cup grated yellow onion

3 cloves garlic, peeled and minced

1 large egg

1 teaspoon paprika

2 teaspoons dried oregano

1 teaspoon salt, divided

¾ teaspoon ground black pepper, divided

2 tablespoons extra-virgin olive oil

3 cups sliced white mushrooms

1 small yellow onion, peeled and diced

2 tablespoons all-purpose flour

¼ cup white wine

2 cups low-sodium chicken broth

1 cup low-fat milk

2 bay leaves

4 sprigs fresh thyme

1 Preheat oven to 425°F. Line a large baking sheet with parchment paper.

2 In a small bowl, place bread and sprinkle with 2 tablespoons water. Crumble bread with your hands into small pieces.

3 In a large bowl, combine crumbled bread, chicken, grated onion, garlic, egg, paprika, oregano, ½ teaspoon salt, and ½ teaspoon pepper. Mix with your hands just until all ingredients are incorporated.

4 Roll mixture into 1" balls and place on prepared baking sheet. Bake meatballs 12 minutes. Remove from oven and set aside.

5 Heat oil in a large skillet over medium heat. Sauté mushrooms 4 minutes. Add diced onion and sauté 5 minutes. Stir in flour and cook 1 minute. Add wine and cook, stirring constantly, 2 minutes. Add broth, milk, bay leaves, thyme, remaining ½ teaspoon salt, and remaining ¼ teaspoon pepper.

6 Stir in meatballs and bring to a boil. Reduce heat to medium-low, cover, and simmer 30 minutes, stirring occasionally.

7 Uncover and cook another 5–6 minutes until sauce has thickened. Remove and discard bay leaves and thyme sprigs. Serve immediately.

Chicken with Okra

This is a traditional Greek dish that's simple to make. Using frozen okra saves on prep time, and you'll find no difference in taste.

1 (3-pound) chicken, cut into 8 pieces

1 teaspoon salt, divided

¾ teaspoon ground black pepper, divided

4 large, very ripe tomatoes

2 tablespoons extra-virgin olive oil

2 large yellow onions, peeled and sliced

2 pounds small okra or 2 (16-ounce) packages thawed frozen baby okra

5 cloves garlic, peeled and sliced

4 whole allspice berries

½ cup chopped fresh parsley

1 Sprinkle chicken pieces with ½ teaspoon salt and ¼ teaspoon pepper. Place in a large stockpot and add just enough water to cover. Bring to a boil over high heat.

2 Reduce heat to medium-low and simmer 30 minutes, skimming the fat from the liquid occasionally. Remove chicken from the pot and transfer to a large baking dish. Reserve the stock.

3 Using a box grater, grate tomatoes into a medium bowl and set aside.

4 Preheat oven to 375°F.

5 Heat oil in a large skillet over medium-high heat. Sauté onions about 7 minutes until translucent. Add okra and sauté 5 minutes. Stir in tomatoes, garlic, allspice berries, parsley, and remaining ½ teaspoon each salt and pepper. Cook, stirring, 5 minutes. Gently stir in 1 cup reserved stock.

6 Transfer okra mixture to the baking dish, covering the chicken, and cover the dish. Bake 30 minutes, then uncover and bake 15 minutes more.

7 Set aside to cool 5 minutes before serving.

SERVES 4

Per Serving:

Calories	200
Fat	7g
Sodium	370mg
Carbohydrates	16g
Fiber	4g
Sugar	7g
Protein	21g

WHOLE CHICKEN

Buying a whole chicken and segmenting it yourself is the most economical choice. But this recipe can be made with bone-in thighs, drumsticks, or breast halves.

Lemon Salmon with Green Beans and Bulgur

Salmon fillets are perfect for weeknight cooking. They're readily available, easy to cook, and delicious!

SERVES 4

Per Serving:

Calories	660
Fat	34g
Sodium	1,340mg
Carbohydrates	48g
Fiber	10g
Sugar	11g
Protein	43g

BULGUR

Bulgur wheat is made from cracked durum wheat and is a great alternative to rice, containing twice the fiber. It's available in fine ground, medium-coarse, and coarse varieties.

4 (6-ounce) skin-on salmon fillets

2 tablespoons grated lemon zest

1¾ teaspoons salt, divided

½ teaspoon ground black pepper, divided

1 tablespoon red wine vinegar

¼ cup minced shallots

1 tablespoon Dijon mustard

1 clove garlic, peeled and minced

1 tablespoon honey

3 tablespoons lemon juice

¼ cup orange juice

3 tablespoons grapefruit juice

3 tablespoons chopped drained capers

8 kalamata olives, sliced

2 teaspoons fresh thyme leaves

6 tablespoons extra-virgin olive oil, divided

1 pound green beans, trimmed

2 cups cooked medium-coarse bulgur

2 tablespoons sliced almonds

1½ teaspoons drained whole capers

1 Spray fillets with nonstick cooking spray and sprinkle with lemon zest, ½ teaspoon salt, and ¼ teaspoon pepper. Set aside 15 minutes.

2 Place vinegar and shallots in a medium glass jar with a lid and set aside 5 minutes. Add mustard, garlic, honey, juices, chopped capers, olives, thyme, 4 tablespoons oil, ¼ teaspoon salt, and remaining ¼ teaspoon pepper. Close the jar and shake vigorously until dressing is emulsified.

3 Fill a large pot with water and place over high heat. Add remaining 1 teaspoon salt and bring to a boil. Add green beans and cook 5 minutes. Drain and rinse under cold water. Transfer to a large bowl.

4 Add bulgur to the bowl with green beans. Pour dressing over bulgur and green beans and stir to combine.

5 Heat remaining 2 tablespoons oil in a large skillet over medium-high heat. Add fillets skin side down. Cook 4 minutes per side.

6 Spoon green bean mixture onto a platter and top with fillets. Garnish with almonds and whole capers and serve.

Chicken Cacciatore

SERVES 6

Per Serving:

Calories	540
Fat	19g
Sodium	800mg
Carbohydrates	21g
Fiber	4g
Sugar	7g
Protein	57g

Chicken Cacciatore is chicken prepared "hunter's style." This means in a tomato-based sauce with onions, bell peppers, and mushrooms. It makes a wonderful Sunday dinner.

½ cup all-purpose flour

1 (3-pound) chicken, cut into pieces

1 teaspoon salt

½ teaspoon ground black pepper

¼ cup extra-virgin olive oil

1 (3-ounce) Italian-style turkey sausage, casing removed

2 medium yellow onions, peeled and diced

1 large carrot, peeled and chopped

1 stalk celery, chopped

⅓ cup diced green bell pepper

1 cup sliced cremini mushrooms

3 bay leaves

2 teaspoons chopped fresh rosemary

1 tablespoon tomato paste

¼ cup chopped fresh parsley

4 cloves garlic, peeled and minced

1 cup dry white wine

1 (28-ounce) can plum tomatoes, hand crushed

½ cup low-sodium chicken broth

1 Place flour in a shallow bowl. Season chicken pieces with salt and black pepper and dredge in flour. Heat oil in a large saucepan or Dutch oven over medium-high heat. Add chicken and brown 5 minutes per side. Remove from pan and set aside.

2 Add sausage to the same pan and cook, breaking it up with a wooden spoon, 3 minutes. Add onions, carrot, celery, bell pepper, mushrooms, bay leaves, and rosemary. Sauté 7 minutes until onions are translucent.

3 Stir in tomato paste, parsley, garlic, and wine. Cook, stirring occasionally, 5 minutes until liquid is reduced by one-third.

4 Return chicken pieces, plus any accumulated juices, to the pan. Add tomatoes and broth and bring to a boil. Reduce heat to low, partially cover the pan, and simmer 60–80 minutes until sauce is thickened and chunky.

5 Remove and discard bay leaves. Serve hot.

Roasted Branzino with Potatoes and Fennel

This easy meal contains all the flavors of the Mediterranean seaside, and it makes a great special occasion splurge meal. Branzino is sometimes called European sea bass in fish markets. Serve with a side of sautéed garlicky greens.

2 small (1-pound) whole branzino

2 tablespoons extra-virgin olive oil, divided

½ teaspoon salt, divided

½ teaspoon ground black pepper, divided

¼ cup fennel fronds, divided

4 small red potatoes, peeled and halved

1 small yellow onion, peeled and sliced

1 cup thinly sliced fennel

1½ tablespoons lemon juice

2 teaspoons grated lemon zest

2 tablespoons chopped fresh parsley

¼ cup dry white wine

½ cup vegetable stock

2 large tomatoes, cored and sliced

4 scallions, trimmed and chopped

4 pitted kalamata olives

2 teaspoons drained and rinsed capers

½ medium lemon, cut into wedges

SERVES 2

Per Serving:

Calories	760
Fat	29g
Sodium	1,110mg
Carbohydrates	88g
Fiber	12g
Sugar	20g
Protein	44g

FENNEL

Fennel has a mild anise flavor and aroma, which complements fish and seafood nicely.

1 Preheat oven to 450°F. Spray a large, deep baking dish with non-stick cooking spray.

2 Brush fish with 1 tablespoon oil. Season inside and out with ¼ teaspoon each salt and pepper. Stuff half of the fennel fronds into the cavities of the fish and set aside.

3 In prepared baking dish, place potatoes, onion, sliced fennel, remaining 1 tablespoon oil, lemon juice, lemon zest, parsley, wine, and stock. Toss to mix and sprinkle with remaining ¼ teaspoon each salt and pepper. Layer tomato slices over the potato mixture. Bake 25 minutes.

4 Remove potato mixture from oven and top with fish. Sprinkle with scallions, olives, and capers. Bake another 20–25 minutes until potatoes are fork-tender and fish is golden brown.

5 Top with remaining fennel fronds before serving with lemon wedges.

Shrimp Giouvetsi

Baked orzo with vegetables and shrimp is sure to be a family favorite.

WATCH THE SHRIMP!

If you pay attention, shrimp will tell you when they're done. Just remember this simple rule: If shrimp form a C shape, they're cooked. If they're in the form of an O, they're overdone.

2 pounds large shrimp, peeled and deveined, shells reserved

4 cups water

¾ teaspoon salt, divided

2 tablespoons extra-virgin olive oil

1½ cups diced yellow onions

4 cloves garlic, peeled and finely chopped

½ cup diced green bell pepper

½ cup diced red bell pepper

¼ cup grated carrot

2 tablespoons tomato paste

2 tablespoons chopped fresh parsley

2 bay leaves

¼ teaspoon ground black pepper

1 cup orzo

¼ cup dry white wine

⅛ teaspoon crushed red pepper flakes

1 teaspoon ground star anise

3 tablespoons chopped fresh dill, divided

1 Place shrimp shells in a large pot with water. Add ½ teaspoon salt and bring to a boil over high heat. Reduce heat to medium-low and simmer 20 minutes. Strain and set aside to cool.

2 Meanwhile, heat oil in a large skillet over medium-high heat. Sauté onions, garlic, bell peppers, and carrot 5–7 minutes until softened. Add tomato paste, parsley, bay leaves, black pepper, and remaining ¼ teaspoon salt. Sauté 1 minute.

3 Add orzo and cook, stirring, 2 minutes until lightly toasted. Stir in wine and cook 1 minute more. Add shrimp stock, red pepper flakes, and star anise and bring to a boil, stirring occasionally. Remove and discard bay leaves.

4 Preheat oven to 375°F.

5 Transfer the contents of the skillet to a 3-quart baking dish. The liquid should be about 1" above the orzo mixture. Add hot water to the baking dish if necessary. Bake 30–35 minutes until most of the liquid has been absorbed.

6 Remove from the oven and stir in 2 tablespoons dill. Place shrimp on top and return dish to the oven. Bake 5 minutes until shrimp are pink and C-shaped.

7 Sprinkle with remaining 1 tablespoon dill before serving.

Sheet Pan Gnocchi and Shrimp

Keep a bag of shelf-stable gnocchi and some frozen shrimp on hand, and you can whip up this simple dinner in minutes. It's so easy to make, and everyone will love it!

1 (16-ounce) package shelf-stable or frozen potato gnocchi

2 tablespoons extra-virgin olive oil

¾ teaspoon salt, divided

¾ teaspoon ground black pepper, divided

2 tablespoons unsalted butter

1 cup minced yellow onion

1 (28-ounce) can plum tomatoes, hand crushed

½ teaspoon ground star anise

¼ teaspoon crushed red pepper flakes

1 pound large shrimp, peeled and deveined

¼ cup grated graviera or Gruyère cheese

¼ cup crumbled feta cheese

¼ cup chopped fresh parsley

SERVES 4

Per Serving:

Calories	560
Fat	20g
Sodium	2,090mg
Carbohydrates	63g
Fiber	4g
Sugar	8g
Protein	28g

1 Preheat oven to 450°F. Line a large baking sheet with parchment paper.

2 In a large bowl, combine gnocchi, oil, ¼ teaspoon salt, and ¼ teaspoon black pepper. Toss to coat. Transfer to prepared baking sheet and spread gnocchi out into a single layer.

3 Bake 10 minutes. Remove from oven and stir gnocchi, then bake another 6–7 minutes until lightly browned.

4 Meanwhile, melt butter in a medium skillet over medium-high heat. Sauté onion 5 minutes, then stir in tomatoes and bring to a boil. Reduce heat to medium-low and simmer 20 minutes or until thickened. Stir in star anise and red pepper flakes. Remove from heat and keep warm.

5 In a large bowl, place shrimp and season with remaining ½ teaspoon each salt and black pepper. Add half the tomato sauce and toss to combine. Pour shrimp mixture over gnocchi. Top with remaining sauce and cheeses. Bake 5–6 minutes until cheese melts.

6 Garnish with parsley before serving.

Slow Cooker Paella

Using a slow cooker to make paella really helps to develop the deep and delicious flavors of this popular Spanish dish.

1½ cups long-grain white rice

1 (14.5-ounce) can diced tomatoes

2¼ cups low-sodium chicken broth

½ teaspoon crushed saffron threads or ½ teaspoon ground turmeric

½ teaspoon smoked paprika

1 tablespoon extra-virgin olive oil

½ pound andouille sausage, halved and sliced

1 medium red onion, peeled and finely diced

6 (3-ounce) boneless, skinless chicken thighs

1 cup thawed frozen baby peas

6 large frozen deveined, peeled, and cooked shrimp

1. In a 4- to 5-quart slow cooker, mix together rice, tomatoes, broth, saffron, and paprika.
2. In a large skillet or Dutch oven over medium heat, heat oil until hot but not smoking. Add sausage and onion and cook until sausage is browned and onion is softened. Using a slotted spoon, transfer sausage and onion to slow cooker and stir well.
3. Increase heat to medium-high and add chicken to the same skillet. Cook until golden brown, about 10 minutes.
4. Place chicken on top of rice mixture. Cover and cook on low 6 hours.
5. Add peas to mixture and stir well. Top with shrimp and cook an additional 30 minutes, until shrimp and peas are cooked through.

SERVES 6

Per Serving:

Calories	440
Fat	16g
Sodium	650mg
Carbohydrates	42g
Fiber	2g
Sugar	3g
Protein	29g

SLOW COOKING WITH SHRIMP

When slow cooking with shrimp, resist the temptation to put the shrimp in at the beginning of the recipe. While it takes longer to overcook foods in the slow cooker, delicate shrimp can go from tender to rubbery very quickly. For most recipes, 20 minutes on high is sufficient cooking time for shrimp.

Cioppino

SERVES 8

Per Serving:

Calories	210
Fat	3.5g
Sodium	1,040mg
Carbohydrates	15g
Fiber	3g
Sugar	6g
Protein	25g

BETTER BUTTER

Set out some delicious herbed or spiced butter next to the bread, potatoes, or vegetables on your table. Blend 1 stick softened butter with 2 tablespoons fresh tarragon, dill weed, or dried rosemary or 2 teaspoons minced garlic or cracked pepper.

This hearty and delicious seafood stew is best served with crusty whole-grain bread to sop up all the juices.

1 medium yellow onion, peeled and chopped

2 stalks celery, diced

6 cloves garlic, peeled and minced

1 (28-ounce) can diced tomatoes

8 ounces clam juice

¾ cup fish stock

1 (6-ounce) can tomato paste

1 teaspoon crushed red pepper flakes

2 tablespoons minced fresh oregano

2 tablespoons minced fresh parsley

1 teaspoon red wine vinegar

10 ounces catfish nuggets

10 ounces large shrimp, peeled and deveined

6 ounces diced cooked clams

6 ounces lump crabmeat

¾ cup diced cooked lobster meat

¼ cup diced scallions

1. Place onion, celery, garlic, tomatoes, clam juice, stock, tomato paste, red pepper flakes, oregano, parsley, and vinegar in a 4- to 5-quart slow cooker. Stir vigorously. Cook on low 8 hours.

2. Add remaining ingredients and cook on high 30 minutes. Stir prior to serving.

Swordfish Souvlaki

Eating fish is a healthy (and delicious) way to wean yourself off red meat. Swordfish is meaty, sustainable, protein-rich, and full of omega-3 fatty acids.

⅓ cup plus ¼ cup extra-virgin olive oil, divided

3 tablespoons lemon juice, divided

1 tablespoon grated lemon zest

1½ teaspoons Dijon mustard, divided

2 cloves garlic, peeled and minced

½ teaspoon fresh thyme leaves

¾ teaspoon ground black pepper, divided

4 (4-ounce) swordfish steaks, skin removed, trimmed of bones and any dark meat and cubed

1 teaspoon chopped drained capers

1 teaspoon dried oregano

1 large red bell pepper, seeded and cut into wedges

1 large green bell pepper, seeded and cut into wedges

1 large red onion, peeled and cut into wedges

1 pint cherry or grape tomatoes

¾ teaspoon salt

½ medium lemon, cut into 4 wedges

SERVES 4

Per Serving:

Calories	360
Fat	24g
Sodium	570mg
Carbohydrates	12g
Fiber	3g
Sugar	7g
Protein	24g

OTHER OPTIONS

Any firm-fleshed fish will work in this recipe. Try monkfish, grouper, mahi-mahi, or halibut. These are larger fish that will make an equally delicious dish.

1 In a large, shallow bowl, whisk together ⅓ cup oil, 1 tablespoon lemon juice, lemon zest, 1 teaspoon mustard, garlic, thyme, and ¼ teaspoon black pepper. Add swordfish and toss to coat. Cover and refrigerate 1 hour.

2 Meanwhile, in a small glass jar with a lid, place remaining ¼ cup oil, remaining 2 tablespoons lemon juice, remaining ½ teaspoon mustard, capers, and oregano. Close the jar and shake vigorously until dressing is emulsified. Set dressing aside.

3 Remove swordfish from refrigerator and let sit about 15 minutes until room temperature.

4 Preheat a charcoal or gas grill. Lightly oil grate.

5 On four large metal skewers, thread fish alternately with bell peppers, onion, and tomatoes. Place skewers on a large platter or baking sheet. Season with salt and remaining ½ teaspoon black pepper.

6 Grill skewers 10 minutes, turning often. Serve with lemon wedges.

CHAPTER 11

Side Dishes

Braised Escarole

Escarole is packed with fiber, has zero fat, and contains vitamins A, C, and K. It's a wonderful side with fish. Add grated Parmesan or Romano cheese to enhance the flavor of the escarole.

SERVES 6

Per Serving:

Calories	140
Fat	3g
Sodium	170mg
Carbohydrates	20g
Fiber	9g
Sugar	3g
Protein	6g

DUTCH OVEN

If you don't have a Dutch oven, don't disregard this recipe. Any deep pot with a heavy bottom and tight-fitting lid can be substituted for a Dutch oven.

1 tablespoon extra-virgin olive oil

3 large heads escarole, cored and torn into bite-sized pieces

2 large leeks, trimmed and sliced

8 cloves garlic, peeled and minced

1 cup drained and rinsed canned cannellini beans

½ cup dry white wine

2 cups vegetable stock

½ teaspoon ground black pepper

1 Heat oil in a large Dutch oven over medium heat. Add escarole, leeks, and garlic; sauté 1 minute. Add beans and wine. Stir and cook 1 minute.

2 Add stock, cover, and simmer 20 minutes. Remove from heat. Season with pepper and serve.

Steamed Broccoli and Cauliflower

This dish is simple and healthy. Steaming is the best way to cook a vegetable and retain most of its nutrients.

1 small head cauliflower, trimmed and cut into florets

1 medium head broccoli, trimmed and cut into florets

¼ cup extra-virgin olive oil

1 tablespoon lemon juice

½ teaspoon salt

¼ cup chopped fresh chives

1 Place cauliflower and broccoli in a steamer basket over simmering water. Cover and steam 8–10 minutes just until tender.

2 In a large bowl, whisk together oil, lemon juice, and salt. Add broccoli and cauliflower and toss gently. Top with chives and serve hot.

SERVES 6

Per Serving:

Calories	100
Fat	9g
Sodium	200mg
Carbohydrates	2g
Fiber	1g
Sugar	1g
Protein	1g

GROW YOUR OWN

Chives are easy to grow in a garden or in a pot on your windowsill. Growing your own means you'll always be able to snip some to add their fresh, mildly oniony flavor to vegetables, fish, or even scrambled eggs.

Zucchini Purée

SERVES 8

Per Serving:

Calories	190
Fat	11g
Sodium	440mg
Carbohydrates	21g
Fiber	4g
Sugar	5g
Protein	6g

FRESH NUTS

Pine nuts can quickly turn rancid if you store them at room temperature. To keep them fresh, store them in the freezer. In fact, you can keep all nuts in the freezer.

Try this when you're looking for a different side dish for dinner. Even the pickiest eaters will enjoy this combination of potatoes and zucchini enriched with Parmesan cheese and pine nuts.

1½ teaspoons salt, divided

2 large russet potatoes, peeled and cubed

8 medium zucchini, trimmed and cut into large pieces

2 tablespoons extra-virgin olive oil

¼ cup grated Parmesan cheese

½ cup pine nuts, lightly toasted

½ cup chopped fresh mint

½ teaspoon ground black pepper

1 Fill a large saucepan with water and add 1 teaspoon salt. Bring to a boil over high heat and add potatoes. Boil 5 minutes, then add zucchini. Cook another 5–6 minutes until potatoes are fork-tender. Remove from heat.

2 Drain and return potatoes and zucchini to the still-warm pan. Add oil, Parmesan, pine nuts, mint, pepper, and remaining ½ teaspoon salt. Mash mixture with a potato masher or a fork.

3 Serve warm.

Horta Vrasta (Boiled Leafy Greens)

In Greece, this dish is made with wild foraged greens. You may be able to find some at a farmers' market. But sturdy greens found at the supermarket work just as well.

1 teaspoon salt

1 bunch Swiss chard, mustard greens, amaranth, Chinese broccoli, or kale, stalks and leaves separated

3 tablespoons extra-virgin olive oil

1½ tablespoons red wine vinegar

2 scallions, trimmed and sliced

2 cloves garlic, peeled and minced

1 teaspoon sesame oil

⅛ teaspoon crushed red pepper flakes

1 teaspoon sesame seeds

1 Fill a large pot with water and add salt. Place over high heat and bring to a boil.

2 Add stalks of greens and boil 2 minutes. Add leaves and boil 1 minute more.

3 Drain greens and transfer to a large bowl. Add olive oil, vinegar, scallions, and garlic and toss to combine.

4 Sprinkle with sesame oil and top with red pepper flakes and sesame seeds before serving.

SERVES 4

Per Serving:

Calories	130
Fat	12g
Sodium	360mg
Carbohydrates	5g
Fiber	2g
Sugar	1g
Protein	2g

Spicy Sesame Broccolini

SERVES 4

Per Serving:

Calories	110
Fat	9g
Sodium	680mg
Carbohydrates	4g
Fiber	0g
Sugar	1g
Protein	4g

WHAT IS BROCCOLINI?

Broccolini is a hybrid of broccoli and gai lan, also called Chinese broccoli. It's milder in taste and crunchier in texture than regular broccoli. Broccolini requires almost no advance preparation. Just trim the bottom inch from a bunch, and you're good to go.

Make this dish as hot or mild as you like by varying the amount or type of hot sauce. Start with a small amount and add more gradually, tasting after each addition. Remember, you can always add more hot sauce, but you can't take it away!

1½ teaspoons salt, divided

1 pound broccolini, trimmed

2 tablespoons extra-virgin olive oil

2 cloves garlic, peeled and minced

2 teaspoons hot pepper sauce

1 teaspoon balsamic vinegar

1 teaspoon sesame oil

1 tablespoon sesame seeds

1   Fill a large saucepan with water and add 1 teaspoon salt. Bring to a boil over high heat, then add broccolini. Boil 2 minutes, then drain and rinse with cool water. Drain again.

2   Heat oil in a large skillet over high heat. Sauté broccolini for 2 minutes, stirring often. Add garlic, hot sauce, and vinegar and sauté 2 minutes more.

3   Remove from heat and sprinkle with sesame seeds and remaining ½ teaspoon salt. Drizzle with sesame oil and serve.

Swiss Chard Gratin

SERVES 4

Per Serving:

Calories	160
Fat	10g
Sodium	770mg
Carbohydrates	12g
Fiber	2g
Sugar	4g
Protein	6g

Swiss chard stems are usually discarded, but this recipe uses both leaves and stems. A béchamel sauce and bread crumb topping make this dish worthy of a special occasion.

1 cup low-fat milk

1½ teaspoons salt, divided

1 bunch Swiss chard, stalks and leaves separated

2 tablespoons extra-virgin olive oil

2 tablespoons all-purpose flour

4 tablespoons grated Asiago cheese, divided

¼ teaspoon ground black pepper

2 tablespoons plain bread crumbs

1 Preheat oven to 375°F. Spray a 9" × 9" baking dish with nonstick cooking spray.

2 Heat milk in a small saucepan over medium-low heat for 2–3 minutes until it just begins to simmer. Keep warm.

3 Fill a large pot with water and add 1 teaspoon salt. Bring to a boil over high heat and add chard stalks. Boil 3–4 minutes until tender. Add leaves and boil 2 minutes more. Drain chard in a colander and set aside.

4 In the same pot over medium heat, heat oil. Add flour and cook, stirring, 1 minute. Slowly add hot milk to the pot, whisking constantly. Cook, stirring, 4–5 minutes until thickened. Remove from heat and add 2 tablespoons Asiago. Stir until smooth.

5 Add chard and stir to coat. Season with pepper and remaining ½ teaspoon salt. Transfer to prepared baking dish. Top with bread crumbs and remaining 2 tablespoons Asiago.

6 Bake 20 minutes or until just golden on top and bubbling. Remove from oven and cool 5 minutes before serving.

Fava Bean and Onion Stifado

According to studies, fava beans contain immune-boosting nutrients. Consuming them may improve blood pressure and aid in weight loss. They're also beneficial for bone health. And they make a tasty stew as well!

2 tablespoons extra-virgin olive oil

2 medium yellow onions, peeled and sliced

3 cloves garlic, peeled and minced

2 (15-ounce) cans fava beans, drained and rinsed

2 cups tomato purée

2 bay leaves

½ teaspoon ground allspice

½ teaspoon salt

½ teaspoon ground black pepper

1 teaspoon dried oregano

1 Heat oil in a medium saucepan over medium-high heat. Sauté onions 5 minutes. Add garlic and sauté 1 minute.

2 Add beans, tomato purée, bay leaves, allspice, salt, and pepper and bring to a boil. Reduce heat to medium-low, cover partially with a lid, and simmer 35 minutes. Stir in oregano.

3 Remove and discard bay leaves before serving.

SERVES 6

Per Serving:

Calories	190
Fat	5g
Sodium	500mg
Carbohydrates	29g
Fiber	2g
Sugar	7g
Protein	10g

Baked Zucchini Patties

SERVES 4

Per Serving:

Calories	290
Fat	19g
Sodium	1,300mg
Carbohydrates	20g
Fiber	2g
Sugar	6g
Protein	11g

This recipe is popular in the summer months, when gardens and local markets are teeming with zucchini. These patties pack well for a road trip or picnic.

3 medium zucchini, trimmed

1½ teaspoons salt, divided

3 tablespoons olive oil, divided

1 cup sliced scallions

1 clove garlic, peeled and minced

1 large egg, lightly beaten

2 tablespoons chopped fresh mint or 1 tablespoon dried mint

1 tablespoon chopped fresh dill

1 tablespoon chopped fresh parsley

¼ cup plain bread crumbs

¼ cup all-purpose flour

1 teaspoon baking powder

¼ cup grated graviera or Gouda cheese

½ cup crumbled feta cheese

½ teaspoon ground black pepper

¼ cup Vegan Yogurt Tzatziki (see recipe in Chapter 5)

1 Using the large holes of a box grater, grate zucchini into a large colander set over a bowl. Sprinkle with 1 teaspoon salt, cover, and refrigerate at least 3 hours.

2 Place zucchini on a large kitchen towel, roll it up, and squeeze out as much liquid as you can. Transfer to a large bowl.

3 Preheat oven to 425°F. Line a large baking sheet with parchment paper and spray it with nonstick cooking spray.

4 Heat 1 tablespoon oil in a small skillet over medium heat. Sauté scallions 3 minutes. Add garlic and sauté 1 minute. Cool 5 minutes, then add scallion mixture to zucchini.

5 Add egg, mint, dill, parsley, bread crumbs, flour, baking powder, cheeses, pepper, and remaining ½ teaspoon salt. Mix with a wooden spoon or your hands until incorporated.

6 Form about 2 tablespoons zucchini mixture into a ball and flatten into a small patty. Place on prepared baking sheet. Repeat with remaining mixture, spacing the patties about 1" apart. Brush the tops of the patties with remaining 2 tablespoons oil.

7 Bake on the lowest oven rack 8 minutes. Flip patties and bake another 8 minutes.

8 Serve warm with Vegan Yogurt Tzatziki.

Roasted Cauliflower with Anchovy Sauce

Cauliflower undergoes a complete transformation when roasted in the oven—the sugars in the vegetable caramelize, and the flavor is sweet and nutty. Add the umami taste of anchovies, creamy tahini, and a burst of acidity from lemon juice, and you have a winning combination.

4 oil-packed anchovy fillets, drained

½ cup tahini

2 tablespoons lemon juice

3 cloves garlic, peeled

¼ teaspoon minced chives

8 cups cauliflower florets

3 tablespoons extra-virgin olive oil

¾ teaspoon salt

¼ teaspoon ground black pepper

½ cup finely chopped fresh parsley

1 Preheat oven to 450°F. Line a large baking sheet with parchment paper.
2 Combine anchovies, tahini, lemon juice, and garlic in a food processor or blender and process until smooth. Add chives and pulse once or twice. Set aside.
3 Place cauliflower on prepared baking sheet. Drizzle with oil and season with salt and pepper. Toss to coat, then spread cauliflower out into a single layer.
4 Bake 25 minutes.
5 Transfer cauliflower to a large platter. Drizzle with anchovy sauce and garnish with parsley before serving.

SERVES 6

Per Serving:

Calories	230
Fat	18g
Sodium	440mg
Carbohydrates	13g
Fiber	4g
Sugar	3g
Protein	7g

Pumpkin Patties

Baked, not fried, these pretty orange patties make a great side dish or lunch.

1 teaspoon salt

1 large russet potato

2 cups canned pumpkin purée

4 scallions, trimmed and thinly sliced

2 cloves garlic, peeled and minced

1 large egg

2 tablespoons chopped fresh mint or 1 tablespoon dried mint

½ cup chopped fresh dill

1 cup crumbled feta cheese

½ teaspoon ground black pepper

¼ cup plain bread crumbs

1 Fill a medium saucepan with water and add salt. Place over high heat and bring to a boil. Carefully add potato. Reduce heat to medium and parboil potato 10 minutes. Remove potato and place in a bowl of ice water. When cool enough to handle, peel off the skin with the dull side of a knife. Coarsely grate the potato into a large bowl.

2 Add pumpkin, scallions, garlic, egg, mint, dill, feta, pepper, and bread crumbs. Mix with a rubber spatula.

3 Preheat oven to 425°F. Spray a baking sheet with nonstick cooking spray.

4 Form about 2 tablespoons pumpkin mixture into a ball and flatten into a small patty. Place on prepared baking sheet. Repeat with remaining mixture, spacing the patties about 1" apart.

5 Spray the tops of the patties with nonstick cooking spray. Bake 10 minutes, then flip and bake another 10 minutes. Serve warm.

SERVES 6

Per Serving:

Calories	170
Fat	7g
Sodium	430mg
Carbohydrates	21g
Fiber	1g
Sugar	5g
Protein	7g

TINY PUMPKIN PATTIES

Make smaller patties for a fun party appetizer. Serve them with low-fat yogurt or Vegan Yogurt Tzatziki (see recipe in Chapter 5) for dipping.

Corn Sticks

SERVES 8

Per Serving:

Calories	100
Fat	4.5g
Sodium	170mg
Carbohydrates	14g
Fiber	2g
Sugar	2g
Protein	2g

This unusual presentation of corn on the cob features a fun shape and lively seasoning. The wedges can also be skewered and grilled for a backyard barbecue party appetizer.

4 large ears corn, shucked

2 tablespoons extra-virgin olive oil

½ teaspoon garlic powder

1 teaspoon chili powder

½ teaspoon salt

¼ teaspoon ground black pepper

¼ cup chopped fresh chives

1 small lime, cut into quarters

1 Preheat oven to 450°F. Line a large baking sheet with parchment paper.

2 Cut 1 ear of corn in half. On a cutting board, stand one half on the cut end and carefully cut through the cob to create four wedges. Repeat with remaining half and remaining ears of corn. Place wedges on prepared baking sheet.

3 In a small bowl, place oil, garlic powder, chili powder, salt, and pepper and stir to combine. Brush oil mixture on the corn wedges.

4 Bake 25–30 minutes until lightly browned. Transfer to a platter and sprinkle with chives. Serve with lime wedges.

Provençal Potato Salad

This potato salad is every bit as flavorful as mayonnaise-based potato salads. When you cook potatoes with the skins on, they retain much of their nutrients and they taste better.

1½ teaspoons salt, divided

1½ pounds baby red potatoes

3 oil-packed anchovy fillets, drained and finely chopped

2 cloves garlic, peeled and minced

1 tablespoon roughly chopped drained capers

¼ cup finely chopped fresh parsley

1 tablespoon chopped fresh tarragon

1 tablespoon Dijon mustard

2 tablespoons red wine vinegar

2 tablespoons minced red onion

¼ teaspoon ground black pepper

¼ cup extra-virgin olive oil

½ cup pitted kalamata olives

SERVES 6

Per Serving:

Calories	200
Fat	13g
Sodium	860mg
Carbohydrates	19g
Fiber	2g
Sugar	0g
Protein	3g

1 Fill a large pot with water and add 1 teaspoon salt. Place over high heat and bring to a boil. Add potatoes. Return to a boil, then reduce heat to medium-low, cover, and simmer 8 minutes until fork-tender. Drain.

2 Cut potatoes in half and place in a large bowl. Gently stir in anchovies, garlic, capers, parsley, and tarragon.

3 In a small bowl, whisk together mustard, vinegar, onion, pepper, and remaining ½ teaspoon salt. Add oil in a stream, whisking constantly. Pour dressing over potato mixture and toss to coat. Add olives.

4 Serve warm or room temperature.

Roasted Red Peppers

SERVES 4

Per Serving:

Calories	140
Fat	8g
Sodium	300mg
Carbohydrates	15g
Fiber	5g
Sugar	10g
Protein	2g

ROASTING WITHOUT A GRILL

Whole bell peppers can be charred and blistered over a gas range or under an oven broiler. Turn them often so they're evenly charred.

These Roasted Red Peppers can be stored in the freezer up to 6 months. To protect the peppers from freezer burn, leave the charred skins on. Thaw the peppers overnight in the refrigerator and peel the charred skins off the peppers before using.

6 large red bell peppers

2 tablespoons extra-virgin olive oil

½ teaspoon salt

1 Brush the grates of a charcoal or gas grill to make sure it is thoroughly clean. Dip a clean tea towel in vegetable oil and wipe the grill surface with oil. Preheat grill.

2 Place peppers on grill and char on all sides, 10–15 minutes. Transfer to a bowl and cover with plastic wrap. Cool 20 minutes. Remove charred skins and discard. Slit the peppers in half; remove and discard the seeds and stems.

3 Slice or chop peppers and place on a serving tray. Drizzle with oil and season with salt. Serve at room temperature.

Dairy-Free Mashed Potatoes

Boiling potatoes in a flavorful stock and mashing them with olive oil means you don't need milk and butter for this luscious side.

6 medium Yukon Gold potatoes, peeled and quartered

1 teaspoon vegetable bouillon

3 scallions, trimmed and thinly sliced

2 tablespoons extra-virgin olive oil

½ teaspoon salt

¼ teaspoon ground black pepper

1 Place potatoes in a large pot and add enough cold water to cover by 1". Add bouillon and place over medium-high heat. Bring to a boil, then reduce heat to medium-low and simmer 10–12 minutes until fork-tender.

2 Place a colander over a large bowl and drain potatoes, reserving cooking liquid in the bowl. Return potatoes to the pot. Add scallions, oil, salt, and pepper and mash with a potato masher. Add reserved cooking liquid ½ cup at a time and continue to mash until potatoes are smooth.

3 Serve immediately.

SERVES 8

Per Serving:

Calories	240
Fat	3.5g
Sodium	150mg
Carbohydrates	49g
Fiber	0g
Sugar	2g
Protein	6g

Lemony Sweet Potatoes with Pomegranate Seeds

SERVES 6

Per Serving:

Calories	400
Fat	3.5g
Sodium	410mg
Carbohydrates	87g
Fiber	13g
Sugar	22g
Protein	7g

REMOVING POMEGRANATE SEEDS WITHOUT STAINING

Pomegranate seeds are wonderful, but they can stain a wooden chopping board. To avoid that, cut the top off the pomegranate, quickly cut it into quarters, and drop the pieces into a large bowl filled with water. Work the seeds out in the water, drain, and discard skins.

Not only is this dish visually stunning, it's healthful and simple to make.

1 teaspoon plus 1 tablespoon extra-virgin olive oil, divided
2 large sweet potatoes, peeled and diced into ½" cubes
1½ tablespoons packed light brown sugar
½ teaspoon ground nutmeg
½ teaspoon ground cinnamon
1 tablespoon lemon juice
½ cup pomegranate seeds
½ teaspoon salt

1 Grease a 4- to 5-quart slow cooker with 1 teaspoon oil. Add sweet potato cubes.
2 In a small bowl, mix remaining 1 tablespoon oil with sugar, nutmeg, and cinnamon. Add to slow cooker and mix well. Cover and cook on low 8 hours.
3 Stir in lemon juice and pomegranate seeds. Sprinkle with salt. Serve immediately.

Oven-Baked Fries

SERVES 8

Per Serving:

Calories	150
Fat	0g
Sodium	520mg
Carbohydrates	33g
Fiber	2g
Sugar	1g
Protein	4g

REMEDY FOR OLD POTATOES

If your potatoes are looking a little tired, revive them. Peel and cut potatoes and place in a colander. Run them under cold water until the water runs clear. Soak them in cold water 30 minutes and drain. The potato pieces will be crisp and ready to use.

Parboiling the potatoes in a mixture of water and baking soda will give you fries with a crisp exterior and fluffy interior.

4 large russet potatoes, peeled and cut into sticks
½ teaspoon baking soda
1½ teaspoons salt, divided

1 Place potatoes in a large bowl and cover with cold water. Set aside 30 minutes, then drain.
2 Preheat oven to 400°F. Line a baking sheet with parchment paper.
3 Transfer potatoes to a large pot and add enough water to cover. Stir in baking soda and 1 teaspoon salt. Bring to a boil over high heat. Reduce heat to medium-low and simmer 5 minutes. Drain.
4 Place potatoes on prepared baking sheet in a single layer. Bake 15–20 minutes until golden brown.
5 Sprinkle fries with remaining ½ teaspoon salt and serve hot.

Smashed Baby Potatoes

Baking soda is an alkali, which means it will raise the pH level of the potato, making it crisp and brown nicely. A little goes a long way.

1½ pounds baby red potatoes

1½ teaspoons salt, divided

½ teaspoon baking soda

3 tablespoons extra-virgin olive oil

½ teaspoon paprika

¼ teaspoon ground black pepper

¼ cup chopped fresh chives

SERVES 6

Per Serving:

Calories	140
Fat	7g
Sodium	590mg
Carbohydrates	16g
Fiber	2g
Sugar	0g
Protein	2g

1 In a large pot, place potatoes, 1 teaspoon salt, and baking soda. Add enough water to cover. Place over high heat and bring to a boil. Reduce heat to medium-low and simmer 8–10 minutes until fork-tender. Drain in a colander and set aside to cool 5 minutes.

2 Preheat oven to 425°F.

3 Transfer potatoes to a large baking sheet. Using a potato masher or your hands, lightly press down on each potato until the skin cracks and the potato flattens slightly. Drizzle with oil.

4 Bake 40–45 minutes until crisp.

5 Sprinkle potatoes with paprika, pepper, and remaining ½ teaspoon salt. Top with chives before serving.

CHAPTER 12

Desserts and Beverages

Byzantine Fruit Medley

SERVES 8

Per Serving:

Calories	195
Fat	0.5g
Sodium	5mg
Carbohydrates	38g
Fiber	4g
Sugar	32g
Protein	1g

Feel free to experiment with the fruits you use in this recipe.

½ cup red wine
½ cup honey
2 medium apples, peeled, cored, and diced
2 medium pears, peeled, cored, and diced
3 medium mandarin or clementine oranges, peeled and sectioned
1 cup pomegranate seeds (from 1 medium pomegranate)

1 In a small saucepan, bring wine and honey to a boil over high heat. Boil 3–4 minutes to evaporate most of the alcohol. Cool 20 minutes.

2 Combine apples, pears, mandarins, and pomegranate seeds in a medium bowl.

3 Pour wine mixture over fruit and refrigerate at least 1 hour. Stir fruit a few times to ensure sauce covers everything. Serve cold.

Poached Pears

Poached Pears are a great make-ahead dessert. Make them in the fall when pears are in season and many varieties are available in the store.

1½ cups sugar

4 cups water

½ cup honey

1 teaspoon vanilla extract

1 (3") cinnamon stick

3 (3" × 1½") strips lemon peel

4 large Bosc or Anjou pears, halved and cored

2 cups plain low-fat Greek yogurt

½ cup Fig, Apricot, and Almond Granola (see recipe in Chapter 2)

1 Set a large, shallow pot that will fit all pear halves in one layer over medium heat. Add sugar, water, honey, vanilla, cinnamon stick, and lemon peel. Simmer 10 minutes.

2 Meanwhile, cut a piece of parchment paper to fit over the top of the pot. Tear or cut a small hole in the middle.

3 Carefully place the pears in the pot. Cover with the parchment paper. Reduce heat to low and simmer pears 15–17 minutes until they can easily be pierced with a knife.

4 Use a slotted spoon to remove pears from the liquid and set aside. Continue simmering the poaching liquid another 15 minutes until thickened. Remove and discard cinnamon stick and lemon peel. Set aside to cool at least 20 minutes.

5 To serve, spoon a dollop of yogurt onto each of eight small plates and top with a pear half. Drizzle with a spoonful of the thickened poaching liquid and top with granola before serving.

SERVES 8

Per Serving:

Calories	370
Fat	3g
Sodium	43mg
Carbohydrates	81g
Fiber	4g
Sugar	71g
Protein	7g

DON'T HAVE GREEK YOGURT?

You can transform regular yogurt into thicker, Greek-style yogurt. Spoon plain yogurt into a sieve over a bowl and set it in the refrigerator overnight. Discard the liquid and transfer the strained yogurt to a covered container.

Roast Plums with Yogurt and Granola

Baked plums take on a complex, sweet flavor, and tart yogurt offers the perfect balance to this simple yet elegant dessert.

½ cup unsalted butter

1 cup packed light brown sugar

½ teaspoon ground star anise or cinnamon

1 teaspoon vanilla extract

¼ cup mavrodaphne wine, port wine, or other fortified wine

8 medium firm plums, pitted and halved

3 cups low-fat plain Greek yogurt

½ cup Fig, Apricot, and Almond Granola (see recipe in Chapter 2)

SERVES 8	
Per Serving:	
Calories	340
Fat	16g
Sodium	50mg
Carbohydrates	43g
Fiber	2g
Sugar	38g
Protein	10g

1 Preheat oven to 400°F.

2 Melt butter in a medium oven-safe skillet over medium heat. Stir in sugar, star anise, vanilla, and wine. Reduce heat to low and simmer 5 minutes.

3 Place the plums in the skillet cut side up. Spoon sauce over plums.

4 Bake plums in the skillet 10–15 minutes until plums are fork-tender but slightly firm. Set aside to cool 10 minutes.

5 To serve, place two plum halves in a shallow bowl and top with yogurt and granola.

Roasted Pears

SERVES 6

Per Serving:

Calories	130
Fat	0g
Sodium	10mg
Carbohydrates	29g
Fiber	5g
Sugar	19g
Protein	2g

Use your favorite light wine with this recipe. Or try it with pear cider or eau-de-vie.

6 medium pears, peeled, halved, and cored

1 cup sweet white wine

1 tablespoon grated lemon zest

1 teaspoon honey

3 ounces low-fat vanilla Greek yogurt

¼ cup chopped fresh mint

1 Preheat oven to 375°F.

2 Place pears cut-side down in a small roasting pan.

3 In a small bowl, whisk together wine, lemon zest, and honey. Pour over pears. Cover and roast 30 minutes. Uncover and roast 10 minutes longer.

4 On each of six plates, place a dollop of yogurt and top with two pear halves. Sprinkle with mint. Serve warm.

Hosafi (Dried Fruit Compote)

Dried fruit makes a healthy snack or, in this case, an easy and delicious compote. Serve with Greek yogurt.

½ cup chopped dried apricots

½ cup chopped dried figs

¼ cup sultana (golden) raisins

¼ cup dark raisins

½ cup chopped pitted prunes

¾ cup honey

3 whole star anise

½ cup roasted unsalted almonds

SERVES 12

Per Serving:

Calories	175
Fat	3g
Sodium	5mg
Carbohydrates	30g
Fiber	2g
Sugar	32g
Protein	2g

1 In a medium bowl, place apricots, figs, sultanas, dark raisins, and prunes. Add enough hot water to cover the fruit. Cover the bowl and set aside 1 hour.

2 Transfer fruit and soaking liquid to a medium saucepan. If necessary, add more water to cover fruit by 1". Stir in honey and star anise and bring just to a boil over medium-high heat. Reduce heat to medium-low and simmer 45 minutes, stirring occasionally.

3 Remove from heat and remove and discard star anise. Stir in almonds. Set aside to cool at least 1 hour.

4 Serve at room temperature or refrigerate in a covered container up to 3 months.

Strawberry Shortcake with Whipped Yogurt

SERVES 12

Per Serving:

Calories	340
Fat	11g
Sodium	105mg
Carbohydrates	49g
Fiber	2g
Sugar	39g
Protein	11g

MINI TRIFLES

For a delightfully pretty party dessert, cut the cake into small cubes and layer the cubes with strawberries and whipped cream in a glass tumbler. Top each with one perfect strawberry.

This indulgent dessert is perfect for a special occasion luncheon. Make it in early summer, when fresh, local strawberries are available.

1 cup all-purpose flour

1 teaspoon baking powder

¼ teaspoon salt

3 large eggs, separated

1 teaspoon white distilled vinegar

1½ cups granulated sugar, divided

6 tablespoons unsalted butter, softened

4 teaspoons vanilla extract, divided

½ cup low-fat milk

5 cups sliced strawberries

4 cups plain whole-milk Greek yogurt

⅔ cup confectioners' sugar

1 Preheat oven to 350°F. Grease a 9" × 13" baking pan. Line the bottom and sides with parchment paper.

2 In a medium bowl, combine flour, baking powder, and salt. Set aside.

3 In a large bowl, using an electric mixer on high speed, beat egg whites and vinegar about 3 minutes until soft peaks form. Gradually add ½ cup granulated sugar and beat until stiff peaks form. Set aside.

4 In a separate large bowl, beat together egg yolks, butter, 1 teaspoon vanilla, and ½ cup granulated sugar 3–4 minutes until light and frothy. Add flour mixture alternately with milk and beat 2 minutes on low speed. Fold in egg whites.

5 Transfer batter to prepared pan. Bake 30–35 minutes until a toothpick inserted in the center comes out clean. Cool in the pan 10 minutes, then remove from the pan and transfer to a wire rack.

6 In a medium bowl, combine strawberries and remaining ½ cup granulated sugar. Set aside 15 minutes.

7 In a large bowl, beat together yogurt, confectioners' sugar, and remaining 3 teaspoons vanilla 5 minutes.

8 To assemble, cut the cake into 24 small pieces. Place one piece on a small plate. Top with a spoonful of strawberries and a dollop of whipped yogurt. Repeat the layers with a second piece of cake on top. Repeat with remaining cake, strawberries, and whipped yogurt. Serve immediately.

Honey-Lemon Chamomile Tea

If you're cutting down on the amount of caffeine in your diet, try this calming and delicious tea. It's also good for soothing an upset stomach.

1 teaspoon dried chamomile flowers

1½ cups water

1 tablespoon honey

1 lemon wedge

1 Boil chamomile and water in a medium saucepan over high heat. Reduce heat to medium and simmer 30 seconds. Remove from heat and allow tea to steep 5 minutes.

2 Pour tea through a strainer into a cup. Add honey and serve hot with lemon wedge.

SERVES 1

Per Serving:

Calories	80
Fat	0g
Sodium	30mg
Carbohydrates	21g
Fiber	2g
Sugar	18g
Protein	1g

Lemon Verbena Tea

Lemon verbena has a mint-lemon aroma that is very soothing. The lemon verbena plant is native to South America. It was brought to Europe in the 17th century by Portuguese and Spanish explorers.

½ cup dried or fresh loose lemon verbena leaves

5 cups water

4 tablespoons honey

½ large lemon, cut into 4 wedges

1 Boil leaves and water in a medium saucepan over high heat. Reduce heat to medium and simmer 5 minutes. Remove from heat and allow tea to steep 5 minutes.

2 Pour tea through a strainer into cups; add 1 tablespoon honey per cup.

3 Serve tea hot with lemon wedges.

SERVES 4

Per Serving:

Calories	70
Fat	0g
Sodium	15mg
Carbohydrates	19g
Fiber	1g
Sugar	18g
Protein	1g

Watermelon Wedges with Feta and Mint

SERVES 6

Per Serving:

Calories	140
Fat	6g
Sodium	65mg
Carbohydrates	1g
Fiber	0g
Sugar	21g
Protein	2g

BALSAMIC GLAZE

Balsamic glaze is available in stores, but you can make your own. Empty a bottle of balsamic vinegar into a medium saucepan, bring to a boil over high heat, then reduce the heat to medium-low and simmer 20–30 minutes until it's reduced by half. Pour the glaze into a squeeze bottle for easy drizzling. Balsamic glaze will keep in the refrigerator up to 1 month.

Watermelon is so refreshing on a hot summer day. It keeps you hydrated, aids in weight loss, and can be eaten on its own, in a salad, or in a smoothie.

6 large wedges seedless watermelon

¼ cup crumbled feta cheese

2 tablespoons chopped fresh mint

1½ tablespoons extra-virgin olive oil

2 tablespoons balsamic vinegar glaze

1 Arrange watermelon slices on a large platter.
2 Sprinkle with feta and mint. Drizzle oil and glaze over the platter and serve.

Fig Compote with Star Anise

Per Serving:

Calories	210
Fat	0g
Sodium	10mg
Carbohydrates	36g
Fiber	3g
Sugar	27g
Protein	1g

NEED CALCIUM AND FIBER?

Fresh or dried, figs are an excellent source of calcium and fiber, as well as many other nutrients. They are also rich in antioxidants and polyphenols.

Dried figs are sweet and jammy and mix well with warm spices. Serve this compote warm or cool with plain yogurt. It's also good over oatmeal for breakfast.

4 ounces dried figs

1 cup mavrodaphne wine, port wine, or other fortified red wine

2 tablespoons honey

6 whole cloves

1 (3") cinnamon stick

1 whole star anise

1 teaspoon vanilla extract

1 (3" × 1½") strip lemon peel

½ teaspoon crushed red pepper flakes

1 Place all ingredients in a medium saucepan over medium heat and bring just to a boil. Reduce heat to low, cover, and simmer 1½ hours.

2 Remove and discard cinnamon stick, star anise, and lemon peel.

3 Serve warm or refrigerate in a covered container up to 3 months.

Lenten Cake

In the Mediterranean region, cakes that don't include dairy or eggs are often served during Lent. But this vegan cake is good any time of the year. If you have rose water, add a tablespoon with the ouzo. It will add a lightly floral scent and flavor.

SERVES 12

Per Serving:

Calories	470
Fat	23g
Sodium	210mg
Carbohydrates	60g
Fiber	3g
Sugar	28g
Protein	6g

3½ cups all-purpose flour

½ teaspoon salt

½ cup ground almonds

1 teaspoon baking powder

1 tablespoon ground cinnamon

¼ teaspoon ground cloves

2 tablespoons grated orange zest

1 tablespoon grated lemon zest

1½ cups orange juice

1 teaspoon baking soda

1 cup granulated sugar

1 cup extra-virgin olive oil

1 ounce ouzo or brandy

¼ cup chopped walnuts

¼ cup dried cranberries

¼ cup chopped dried cherries

¼ cup raisins

¼ cup toasted sesame seeds

2 tablespoons confectioners' sugar

1 Preheat oven to 350°F. Grease and flour a Bundt pan.

2 In a large bowl, place flour, salt, almonds, baking powder, cinnamon, cloves, orange zest, and lemon zest and mix well.

3 In a small bowl, combine orange juice and baking soda. Pour into flour mixture along with granulated sugar, oil, and ouzo. Stir until just combined. Fold in walnuts, cranberries, cherries, raisins, and sesame seeds.

4 Pour batter into prepared pan and bake 45 minutes until a toothpick inserted into the center comes out clean.

5 Cool in the pan 5 minutes, then carefully invert the cake onto a wire rack. Set aside until completely cool, at least 1 hour.

6 Transfer to a cake plate and dust with confectioners' sugar.

Pear Croustade

A croustade is a French tart. Sweet, ripe pears are tossed in a lightly spiced mixture and baked atop a homemade crust.

SERVES 8

Per Serving:

Calories	260
Fat	9g
Sodium	55mg
Carbohydrates	40g
Fiber	3g
Sugar	17g
Protein	4g

1½ cups plus 1 tablespoon all-purpose flour, divided

7 tablespoons sugar, divided

⅛ teaspoon salt

6 tablespoons cold unsalted butter, cut into ½" pieces

1 large egg yolk

6 tablespoons plain low-fat yogurt

2 large firm but ripe Bosc or Anjou pears, peeled, cored, and cut into thin wedges

1 tablespoon lemon juice

1 teaspoon anise seeds

⅓ teaspoon ground allspice

1 large egg white, lightly beaten

1 Place 1½ cups flour, 3 tablespoons sugar, and salt in food processor. Add butter and pulse until the mixture resembles coarse crumbs. Add egg yolk and pulse 2–3 times. Add yogurt 1 tablespoon at a time and pulse until absorbed.

2 Transfer dough to a floured work surface and form it into a flat disc. Wrap dough in plastic wrap and refrigerate 30 minutes.

3 Preheat oven to 400°F. Line a baking sheet with parchment paper.

4 Roll out dough on floured parchment paper to a 12" round. Transfer to prepared baking sheet.

5 In a large bowl, toss pears with 3 tablespoons sugar, remaining 1 tablespoon flour, lemon juice, anise, and allspice. Spread pear mixture on the center of the dough circle, leaving a 2" border.

6 Fold the edges of the dough over the outside edges of the fruit to create a rim (the center of the pears will be uncovered), crimping slightly as you go. Brush dough with egg white and sprinkle with remaining 1 tablespoon sugar.

7 Bake about 40 minutes until crust is golden and filling bubbles. Cool 15 minutes.

8 Slide a large metal spatula under the crust and transfer to a large plate. Serve warm or at room temperature.

Apple Tart

Firm apples like the Granny Smith variety are ideal for tarts because they hold up well in the heat of the oven. A puff pastry tart like this is so easy to make, but it will wow your guests.

1 sheet thawed frozen puff pastry

4 large Granny Smith apples, peeled, cored, and thinly sliced

¼ cup granulated sugar

¼ cup packed light brown sugar

1 teaspoon ground cinnamon

½ cup unsalted butter, cut into small pieces

½ cup apricot jam

2 tablespoons brandy

SERVES 8	
Per Serving:	
Calories	290
Fat	13g
Sodium	35mg
Carbohydrates	41g
Fiber	3g
Sugar	31g
Protein	1g

1 Preheat oven to 400°F. Line a large baking sheet with parchment paper.

2 Place puff pastry on prepared baking sheet. Place a row of over-lapping apple slices diagonally down the middle. Continue to make diagonal overlapping rows on both sides of the middle row.

3 Sprinkle with granulated sugar, brown sugar, and cinnamon. Dot the apple slices with butter pieces.

4 Bake 50–60 minutes until pastry is golden brown and apples are fork-tender and golden.

5 Melt jam in a small saucepan over medium heat. Remove from heat and stir in brandy.

6 Brush jam mixture over apples while still warm. Set aside to cool at least 20 minutes before serving.

Cantaloupe Granita

In the summer, cantaloupe melons are easy to find anywhere you shop. Bring home an extra melon or two to make this easy and refreshing granita.

2 cups cubed cantaloupe
¼ cup sugar
2 teaspoons lemon juice
¼ cup chopped fresh mint

1 Place all ingredients in a blender and purée until smooth.
2 Pour into a 13" × 9" metal baking pan and freeze 1 hour until mixture forms a slushy consistency.
3 Scrape granita with a fork and scoop into chilled martini glasses or small dessert bowls. Serve immediately.

SERVES 4

Per Serving:

Calories	80
Fat	0g
Sodium	15mg
Carbohydrates	20g
Fiber	1g
Sugar	18g
Protein	1g

CANTALOUPE NUTRITION

One serving of cantaloupe will provide you with 100 percent of your daily requirement for both vitamins A and C. It's also a good source of potassium. And at only 53 calories per cup, it's an appealing and healthful snack.

Apricot and Walnut Tart

SERVES 6

Per Serving:

Calories	250
Fat	8g
Sodium	5mg
Carbohydrates	42g
Fiber	3g
Sugar	20g
Protein	5g

Any type of jam can be used in this recipe. Also, try other kinds of nuts, such as almonds or pecans, to create different flavors.

1 cup flour

2 teaspoons extra-virgin olive oil

1 teaspoon ice water

2 cups chopped apricots

½ cup chopped walnuts

½ cup red currants

¼ cup apricot jam

¼ cup packed light brown sugar

1 Preheat oven to 375°F. Spray a baking sheet with nonstick cooking spray.

2 In a medium bowl, mix together flour, oil, and water to form dough. On a floured surface, roll out dough into a 10" square and place on the prepared baking sheet.

3 In a large bowl, stir together apricots, walnuts, currants, jam, and sugar. Pour mixture onto the center of the dough. Fold edges of dough over filling to within 2" of the center. Fold back corners to leave an opening in center. Bake 30 minutes.

Berries and Meringue

A perfect ending to a picnic, this meringue provides a sweet, light finish to any summer lunch. If you like, stir a few tablespoons of sugar into the berries about 15–30 minutes before serving.

6 large egg whites

½ cup sugar

¼ teaspoon cream of tartar

2 cups fresh berries (blueberries, blackberries, raspberries, or a combination)

1 Preheat oven to 200°F. Line a baking sheet with parchment paper or spray with nonstick cooking spray.

2 In a large copper or stainless steel bowl, using an electric mixer on high speed, beat egg whites, sugar, and cream of tartar until stiff peaks form. Drop egg white mixture onto baking sheet 2" apart to form twelve small mounds. Bake 1½–1¾ hours until dry, crispy, and lightly golden.

3 Place each meringue on a dessert plate. Top with berries.

SERVES 12

Per Serving:

Calories	60
Fat	0g
Sodium	30mg
Carbohydrates	12g
Fiber	1g
Sugar	11g
Protein	2g

Lenten Biscotti

SERVES 24

Per Serving:

Calories	180
Fat	10g
Sodium	15mg
Carbohydrates	20g
Fiber	1g
Sugar	7g
Protein	3g

AN ANCIENT TRADITION

Twice-baked cookies, called "biscotti" by the Italians and "paxima-dia" by the Greeks, have roots in ancient times, when mariners baked pieces of bread twice so they would keep during a long voyage.

These not-too-sweet, nutty biscotti are made without eggs, and they're popular during Lent in the Mediterranean region. But you can make them anytime you want to have a small treat with a cup of tea.

¾ cup vegetable oil

½ cup dry white wine

¼ cup orange juice

1½ tablespoons grated orange zest

¾ cup sugar

1½ teaspoons ground cinnamon

¼ teaspoon ground cloves

¼ teaspoon baking soda

1½ tablespoons baking powder

½ cup roasted almonds

3 cups all-purpose flour

½ cup sesame seeds

1 Preheat oven to 350°F. Line a large baking sheet with parchment paper.

2 Place oil, wine, orange juice, orange zest, sugar, cinnamon, cloves, baking soda, and baking powder in a food processor and pulse until combined. Add almonds and pulse again until almonds are roughly chopped.

3 Transfer mixture to a large bowl and gradually add flour, mixing with your hands. The dough should be smooth and not sticky. Gather dough into a ball and place on a floured work surface.

4 Divide dough into 3 pieces and form each into an oval loaf. Press sesame seeds onto the outsides of all three loaves. Place loaves on prepared baking sheet.

5 Bake 30 minutes. Remove from oven and reduce oven temperature to 300°F.

6 Use a serrated knife to quickly cut the loaves into ¾" slices. Place each slice flat on the baking sheet and return the baking sheet to the oven. Bake 10 minutes. Turn off the heat and leave the baking sheet in the oven 45 minutes.

7 Serve immediately or cool and store in an airtight container up to 6 weeks.

Drunken Biscotti

With only an ounce of ouzo in the dough, these cookies are not overly boozy. But if you prefer, you can substitute $^1/2$ teaspoon anise extract for the ouzo.

4 cups all-purpose flour

1 teaspoon baking powder

1 cup vegetable oil

1 ounce ouzo

1 cup sugar

2 teaspoons vanilla extract

3 tablespoons cracked anise seeds

1 cup roughly chopped roasted unsalted almonds

3 large eggs, lightly beaten

SERVES 24	
Per Serving:	
Calories	230
Fat	13g
Sodium	10mg
Carbohydrates	26g
Fiber	1g
Protein	4g
Sugar	9g

1 Preheat oven to 350°F. Line a large baking sheet with parchment paper.

2 In a medium bowl, combine flour and baking powder.

3 In a large bowl, combine oil, ouzo, sugar, vanilla, anise seeds, almonds, and eggs. Use your hands to mix until incorporated. Add flour mixture and knead 5 minutes. The dough should be soft. Divide dough into three portions and form each into a long oval loaf on prepared baking sheet.

4 Bake 30 minutes. Remove from oven and reduce oven temperature to 300°F.

5 Use a serrated knife to quickly cut the loaves into ¾" slices. Place each slice flat on the baking sheet and return the baking sheet to the oven. Bake 10 minutes. Turn off the heat and leave the baking sheet in the oven 45 minutes.

6 Serve immediately or cool and store in an airtight container up to 6 weeks.

Tahini and Honey Ice Cream

SERVES 8

Per Serving:

Calories	340
Fat	18g
Sodium	50mg
Carbohydrates	43g
Fiber	2g
Sugar	34g
Protein	6g

AMARETTO ANTIFREEZE

Adding a small amount of alcohol to the ice cream means it will not freeze into a solid block. And Amaretto adds a lovely almond flavor to this vegan treat.

Tahini is made of ground sesame seeds and is full of healthy fats, nutrients, and vitamins. It is also a great substitute for peanut butter.

2 cups unsweetened almond milk

1 tablespoon vanilla extract

1 cup tahini

½ cup confectioners' sugar

1 ounce amaretto liqueur

¾ cup honey, divided

2 tablespoons sesame seeds

1 Place the bowl of an ice cream maker in the freezer.
2 Place milk, vanilla, tahini, sugar, amaretto, and ½ cup honey in a medium bowl. Stir to combine, then cover and refrigerate at least 4 hours.
3 Pour the chilled mixture into an ice cream maker and continue according to the manufacturer's directions. Scrape mixture into a covered plastic container and freeze at least 2 hours before serving.
4 Scoop ice cream into bowls and drizzle with remaining ¼ cup honey. Sprinkle with sesame seeds and serve immediately.

Café Frappé

SERVES 1

Per Serving:

Calories	70
Fat	2.5g
Sodium	50mg
Carbohydrates	6g
Fiber	0g
Sugar	7g
Protein	4g

Frappé is among the most popular drinks in Greece, and it's available at virtually all Greek cafés. Add a shot of ouzo to your afternoon frappé!

1 tablespoon instant coffee

1 teaspoon sugar

1 tablespoon room-temperature water

½ cup cold water

2 tablespoons evaporated milk

1. Put coffee, sugar, and room-temperature water into a cocktail shaker and cover. Shake vigorously for 30 seconds.
2. Pour mixture into a tall glass with a few ice cubes. Add enough cold water to almost fill the glass.
3. Add milk and serve immediately with a straw.

Greek Coffee

SERVES 1

Per Serving:

Calories	40
Fat	1g
Sodium	10mg
Carbohydrates	7g
Fiber	1g
Sugar	2g
Protein	1g

A briki is a special one-handled pot used for making Greek Coffee. It comes in various sizes and can be found in Greek or Middle Eastern shops. The grounds will remain at the bottom of the cup. Sip only until you detect a bit of the grounds.

½ cup cold water

1 tablespoon Greek coffee

½ teaspoon sugar

1. Using a demitasse cup, measure the amount of cold water needed to make a serving of coffee. Put water, coffee, and sugar in a briki.
2. Place briki over medium heat. Swirl briki until coffee and sugar dissolve. As soon as coffee foams, remove from heat and pour into cup.
3. Before drinking, let coffee sit about 1 minute to allow the grounds to settle to the bottom of the cup.

STANDARD US/METRIC MEASUREMENT CONVERSIONS

VOLUME CONVERSIONS

US Volume Measure	Metric Equivalent
⅛ teaspoon	0.5 milliliter
¼ teaspoon	1 milliliter
½ teaspoon	2 milliliters
1 teaspoon	5 milliliters
½ tablespoon	7 milliliters
1 tablespoon (3 teaspoons)	15 milliliters
2 tablespoons (1 fluid ounce)	30 milliliters
¼ cup (4 tablespoons)	60 milliliters
⅓ cup	90 milliliters
½ cup (4 fluid ounces)	125 milliliters
⅔ cup	160 milliliters
¾ cup (6 fluid ounces)	180 milliliters
1 cup (16 tablespoons)	250 milliliters
1 pint (2 cups)	500 milliliters
1 quart (4 cups)	1 liter (about)

WEIGHT CONVERSIONS

US Weight Measure	Metric Equivalent
½ ounce	15 grams
1 ounce	30 grams
2 ounces	60 grams
3 ounces	85 grams
¼ pound (4 ounces)	115 grams
½ pound (8 ounces)	225 grams
¾ pound (12 ounces)	340 grams
1 pound (16 ounces)	454 grams

OVEN TEMPERATURE CONVERSIONS

Degrees Fahrenheit	Degrees Celsius
200 degrees F	95 degrees C
250 degrees F	120 degrees C
275 degrees F	135 degrees C
300 degrees F	150 degrees C
325 degrees F	160 degrees C
350 degrees F	180 degrees C
375 degrees F	190 degrees C
400 degrees F	205 degrees C
425 degrees F	220 degrees C
450 degrees F	230 degrees C

BAKING PAN SIZES

American	Metric
8 × 1½ inch round baking pan	20 × 4 cm cake tin
9 × 1½ inch round baking pan	23 × 3.5 cm cake tin
11 × 7 × 1½ inch baking pan	28 × 18 × 4 cm baking tin
13 × 9 × 2 inch baking pan	30 × 20 × 5 cm baking tin
2 quart rectangular baking dish	30 × 20 × 3 cm baking tin
15 × 10 × 2 inch baking pan	30 × 25 × 2 cm baking tin (Swiss roll tin)
9 inch pie plate	22 × 4 or 23 × 4 cm pie plate
7 or 8 inch springform pan	18 or 20 cm springform or loose bottom cake tin
9 × 5 × 3 inch loaf pan	23 × 13 × 7 cm or 2 lb narrow loaf or pate tin
1½ quart casserole	1.5 liter casserole
2 quart casserole	2 liter casserole

Index